HORIZONTAL ANDVERTICAL

Meeting the Global Talent Challenge

Michael F. Tucker & Lori Tucker-Eccher

Manuscript Design and Production
Jodi Tucker-Young

authorHOUSE®

AuthorHouse™
1663 Liberty Drive
Bloomington, IN 47403
www.authorhouse.com
Phone: 1 (800) 839-8640

Published by AuthorHouse 07/21/2017

ISBN: 978-1-5246-9903-1 (sc)
ISBN: 978-1-5246-9901-7 (hc)
ISBN: 978-1-5246-9902-4 (e)

Library of Congress Control Number: 2017910553

Print information available on the last page.

CONTENTS

INTRODUCTION: Why you should read this Book vii

    Global Leadership Gap viii
    The HV Model ix
    Structure of the Book ix
    Background and Motivation of the Authors x

CHAPTER 1: Horizontal Assessment 1

CHAPTER 2: Verification and Self Recognition 7

CHAPTER 3: Vertical Development of the Competencies 10

CHAPTER 4: Developing a Growth Mindset and Managing
    Transitions 40

CHAPTER 5: *THE STUDIES:*
    Identifying the Key Competencies That Are
    Critical For Successful Global Leaders 44

    STUDY ONE: Leading Across Cultures in the Human
    Age: An Empirical Investigation of Intercultural
    Competency Among Global Leaders 45

    STUDY TWO: Additional Research – A Nine
    Competency Model 90

CHAPTER 6: Conclusion 91

REFERENCES 93

ABOUT THE AUTHORS 103

Why You Should
Read This Book

"Cultural issues will dominate the new competencies that will be required for global leaders over the next ten years." (Training Magazine, 2011)

This book is written to answer the following questions...

Can I benchmark myself against other business leaders who work across cultures?

As a high-potential, emerging global leader, what competencies do I need to have and how do I develop them?

Leadership development programs are not producing the effective global leaders that we need. What is new and different about the approach presented in this book?

Global leadership research that has been done leaves a lot to be desired. What is new and different about this research?

This book is designed for all those who are engaged in global business leadership and its development. This includes incumbent leaders, emerging leadership talent, human resource managers engaged in leadership development programs and researchers who study in this area. As the book makes clear, there is a great need for more effective global leadership and new leadership development programs. We present a new model for global leadership assessment and development that combines a competency approach with a self-development one.

Global Leadership Gap

Global business leadership is in a crisis, both in terms of the need for definitive research on the subject as well as the need for statistically valid and applicable assessment and development programs that enhance the ability of leaders who can work effectively across cultures. Studies documenting this crisis, fully described in Chapter 6, include those by IBM, DDI, Right Management and the Chally Group, McKinsey, Training Magazine and the Wall Street Journal.

The field of global leadership research is relatively new and emerging (Mendenhall et al 2008).The studies that have been done provide some insight into what is required for global leadership success, but they also point to a number of areas that need to be better addressed, including representative samples of real-time leaders of different nationalities and a concise set of competencies that can predict success over time. The studies reported in this book address these issues and produce a set of nine validated competencies that are amenable to development, such as Open-mindedness, Navigating Ambiguity and Instilling Trust. The identification and assessment of these nine competencies is a critical first step toward development. They are the "H" (Horizontal) in our new HV Model.

But what are the next steps? Can these competencies be changed and developed? The answer is yes, and that is the "V" or vertical development portion of the HV Model. In order to achieve vertical development, we have taken a cognitive development approach and integrated these nine key competencies into a Change Mapping process (Kegan and Lahey (2009). When a Change Map is created for each competency, these maps can be a highly effective method toward growth and development.

We agree with Petrie (2011) who makes the case in a White Paper for the Center for Creative Leadership that what is needed is both a competency approach and a cognitive development approach focused on mental complexity. Our HV Model of global leadership assessment and development introduced in this book is a refreshing new way of combining these two approaches.

The HV Model

Our HV model for a combined horizontal and vertical approach to developing global leaders appears below in Figure 1. Our model has the horizontal axis based on our empirical research on intercultural competencies as reported in Chapter 5, while the vertical axis builds on the work of Kegan and Lahey (2009) in creating behavior change maps for these competencies as reported in Chapter 3.

In the following chapters of this book, we first target the assessment and development of individual competencies and then place them into the framework of behavior change maps.

Figure 1:

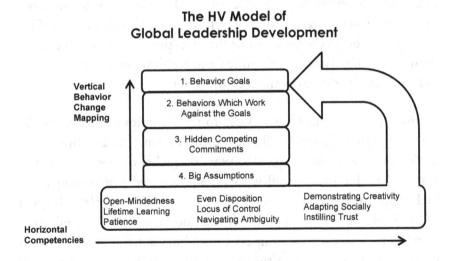

Structure of the Book

We begin in Chapter One by describing our approach to horizontal competency assessment. Our Nine Competency Model is presented and discussed, featuring intercultural competencies as reported in Chapter 3 which predict leadership success over time. These competencies appear in a sample of our Global Leader TAP® Assessment Profile. Chapter Two is a discussion of how we verify and begin development of the Horizontal competencies. Chapter Three is a presentation of Vertical development of the competencies by means of Behavioral Change Mapping, including application cases. A short discussion of how a Growth Mindset applies to development begins Chapter Four, followed by an explanation of how development can be accelerated by managing Mindset Change and Transition. Chapter Five presents our empirical studies of global leadership which produced our Nine Competency Model. A concluding statement in Chapter Six is followed by References.

Background and Motivation of the Authors

The lead author is the founder and President of Tucker International, a full service global consulting organization. He has lived or worked in some 45 countries, leading organizations himself as well as assessing, coaching and developing leaders. As a Ph.D., I/O Psychologist, he has successfully merged academic research scholarship with practical field applications for his clients. Some of the cases presented in Chapter 3 are drawn from Dr. Tucker's assessment and coaching experiences as well as from the experiences of the second author.

Beginning with consulting services to the American Peace Corps in Iran, Afghanistan, the Caribbean, Central America and Brazil, his work has focused for the past 40 years on global corporate managers and leaders. He has worked with several hundred global companies, including at the same time eight of the top ten Fortune 500. The goal of his work, and this book, is to provide solid research and application to produce better global business leadership. But the goal is also to continue a long-term commitment to world peace through international commerce, led by interculturally competent leaders.

Lori Tucker-Eccher is the Director as well as lead Assessor and Executive Coach at Tucker International. She lived as an expatriate as a child and has been involved in the field of intercultural communication in varying capacities for over 20 years.

She is the author of Tucker International's International Mobility Assessment IMA® and architect of Tucker International's *ExpaTracks* (an on-line expatriate candidate assessment tracking system). She is a certified assessor for the Overseas Assignment Inventory (OAI), the TAP® Assessment Profile and the Global Leader TAP® Assessment Profile (GLTAP). She has conducted well over 350 assessment feedback and coaching sessions with expatriates from multi-national companies taking on key leadership roles in over 25 countries. She is particularly interested in exploring research based applications for coaching and developing global leaders and more specifically the methods that inspire motivation for change.

CHAPTER 1

Horizontal Assessment

As stated earlier, we agree with Petri (2011) that both a traditional competency approach and a cognitive development approach focused on mental complexity is needed to provide the type of leadership equal to the challenges presented by the contemporary, increasingly complex global environment. As suggested in Petrie's white paper (2011), "it is time to transcend and include" a leadership competency mentality so that in the future we are able to grow our leaders with required skills. Petrie's approach includes competencies, which he describes as horizontal assessment and development, and suggests they can be "transformed" or learned from an expert. Horizontal learning, the development of new skills, abilities and behaviors, is most useful when a problem is clearly defined and there are known techniques for solving it. It has been and remains an essential part of leadership development.

The first step in our approach is to assess the competencies listed below. They are based on an empirical study by Tucker et al. (2014) which is reported in chapter 5.

Intercultural Competencies

The nine Intercultural Competencies are assessed by means of the Global Leader Tucker Assessment Profile (GLTAP). The competencies are grouped in three clusters; World View, Situational Approach, and Social/Interpersonal Style. Each competency is described below, with a sample of the items in the GLTAP that comprise each one.

WORLD VIEW

Open-Mindedness

Being receptive to and nonjudgmental of the ideas and ways of other countries, cultures, and ethnic groups and demonstrating respect for diverse spiritual and political beliefs.

Sample item: I seek out and enjoy people who are different from me and who have different ideas and opinions.

Lifetime Learning

A pattern of learning over time, reading newspapers and periodicals (in print or electronically), viewing national and international news broadcasts, and attending formal learning sessions.

Sample item: It is a habit of mine to learn from a variety of sources.

SITUATIONAL APPROACH

Patience

The ability to be patient in the face of unanticipated delays or frustrating situations and with people who do not meet expectations of time.

Sample item: I remain calm when I have to wait for other people.

Even Disposition

The ability to remain calm, not be critical of himself or herself, and learn from mistakes.

Sample item: I take things as they come and do not get down on myself.

Navigating Ambiguity

The ability to see through vagueness and uncertainty, not become overly frustrated, and eventually figure out how things are done. Taking the initiative and leading through difficult situations.

> Sample item: I am comfortable with situations involving uncertainty or unexpected outcomes.

Locus of Control

The belief that one's own actions and abilities play a direct role in the process and outcome of the events in life instead of relying on fate, luck or circumstance. Taking responsibility for actions.

> Sample item: Throughout my life, no matter what I did, events seemed to run their own course. (reverse scored).

Demonstrating Creativity

Enjoying new challenges, striving for innovative solutions to social and situational issues, and the ability to see around corners, predict outcomes and act despite uncertainty.

> Sample item: I like to experiment and try out new ways of doing things instead of staying with familiar methods.

SOCIAL/INTERPERSONAL STYLE

Adapting Socially

Being comfortable in new and unfamiliar social settings, seeking out and enjoying diverse groups of people, and showing genuine interest in others.

Sample item: I enjoy meeting strangers and getting to know them.

Instilling Trust

Valuing trust, being seen as someone who can be trusted, and building trusting relationships.

Sample item: Most people cannot be relied on to follow through with their promises (reverse scored)

Success Criteria

In order to link intercultural competencies and to validate them against global leadership performance, three performance areas, or global leader success criteria, were defined and measured in the study described in Chapter 5. These criteria were predicted over time by the competencies.

- *Global Networking:* The demonstrated ability to develop a network of international relationships and make a successful transition to work with people of other nationalities.

  Sample item: I have developed a network of international relationships that help me to succeed with my work.

- *Driving Performance:* The demonstrated ability to provide objective evidence of effectiveness in a global leadership role, team achievement of global business goals, company success in countries of operation, and proof that the company is seen as a preferred place to work.

Sample item: Performance data indicates that my team has achieved our global business objectives.

- *Building Team Effectiveness:* The demonstrated ability to successfully coach team members build trust and a culture of respect, and learn from the team.

    Sample item: I have been able to build trust among my global team. I can rely on them and they on me.

Figure 2 represents our competency model, showing each competency and the separate criteria of leadership success.

Figure 2:

Nine Competency Model
Based on 1880 global leaders of 9 nationalities

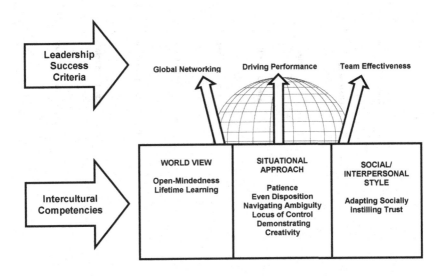

Global Leader TAP® Assessment Profile

A sample GLTAP Profile is shown next in Figure 3. The grey band is a global norm, based on a sample of 1880 global leaders (mean plus or minus ½ S. D.) described in Chapter 5. An individual set of responses is plotted against this norm.

Figure 3:

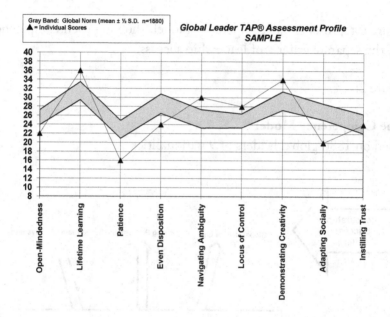

CHAPTER 2

Verification and Self Recognition:

The Connection between the Identification and Development of Horizontal Competencies

The Global Leader TAP® Assessment Profile (GLTAP) provides a reliable and valid way to assess nine key competencies of successful global leaders compared to a database. But where do we go from here to develop these competencies? The next step is the critical phase between identification and change. In order to proceed from this data to behavior change we need to complete the horizontal development phase and be prepared for the vertical phase of development by achieving the following:

- Establish verification, to ensure that the results are a fair and accurate reflection of the person illustrated in the sample.

- Achieve self-recognition. Development is more successful when individuals are able to "see themselves in their scores" and accept that these scores are an accurate reflection of their current strengths or developmental areas.

- Establish motivation for change. Define why recognition and development matters and how it can improve performance.

- Acknowledge the potential for change and emphasize that these "skills are learnable" (Dweck, 2006). An individual's current, measured competencies are not static. Each person can change and develop the areas measured.

Horizontal development is done when a certified coach completes a behavioral interview to verify an individual's results and initiate the development of their competencies through feedback and by inspiring self-recognition.

For example, to verify a very low score on the Patience competency (as in the GLTAP Profile sample given in Figure 3), a behavioral question might be "Please think about a time when things did not proceed as you had planned or a time when you became frustrated with a situation. What happened, how did you feel and what did you do?" A person with a low score in this area might respond by saying, "I get very frustrated when people are late to meetings." Or, they may say, "I feel my time is wasted in meetings where it takes too long for others to make a decision when the solution to the problem seems very obvious to me." Later when the coach provides feedback they can reflect on these answers to illustrate why these responses might reflect an individual who is low on patience. They can then discuss how the perception of time can differ across cultures or how emotions that evolve from feeling impatient can negatively affect interactions. Or, they can explain how being patient, listening and encouraging others to take the time they need to come to a solution is a much more effective leadership strategy than dictating a solution (even if that solution is the very one that they had in mind).

The area of Open-Mindedness is another example of a potential opportunity for development based on the low GLTAP score in Figure 3. In this case a coach may ask the individual if they have ever "had an experience when they observed or interacted with someone from a different culture and they expressed beliefs or engaged in behavior that was very different from what they were used to? What was the situation? How did you react? What was the outcome?" Individual responses to these questions are varied and often informative. One respondent noted how he felt somewhat offended when attending a conference in the Middle East and people would walk away from the meeting at certain times during the day to pray on a prayer rug provided at the back of the room.

Discovering and discussing examples like these with the individual during feedback can be a very powerful method for inspiring self-recognition. The coaching discussion can then turn toward why this area is important for successful global leaders. Most importantly, you can establish that this competency can be developed and that there is potential for change. An attempt is made at the outset to set the stage for the individual to have "a growth mindset" (Dweck, 2006). As a whole, the process combines to create the motivation to change and the ripe opportunity for vertical development.

CHAPTER 3

Vertical Development of the Competencies

Vertical development of the competencies in this book is based in part on Robert Kegan's constructive developmental theory (1982, 1994), which builds on the work of Jean Piaget, Lawrence Kohlberg, William Perry, and others. Kegan's theory of adult cognitive development defines five stages of mental complexity or "orders of mind" that represent five successive levels or stages of more complex ways of thinking (Pruyn 2010).

The stages are the impulsive mind, found in 2-6 year olds; the instrumental mind, found in 6 year olds through adolescence; the socialized mind, found in post-adolescence; the self-authoring mind may occur at variable ages; and the self-transforming mind, found beyond 40 years, if achieved. It is the fifth stage that concerns us here and that differentiates our approach. Less than 1% of adults have achieved the "Level 5" mental complexity of the self-transforming mind (Kegan, R., 1994; Torbert, 1987). This is the ability to step back from and reflect on the limits of our own ideology or personal authority, see that any one system or self-organization is in some way partial or incomplete, be friendlier toward contradiction and opposites and seek to hold on to multiple systems rather than projecting all but one onto the other" (Kegan & Lahey, 2009).

This fifth level of complexity is contrasted with the third and fourth levels, the socialized mind and the self-authoring mind. The socialized mind operates within the perceived social environment or "schools of thought" with which one identifies. Here, information flow is strongly influenced by what one believes others want to hear. At the level of the self-authoring mind, "we are able to step back enough from

10

the social environment to generate an internal seat of judgment or personal authority" (Kegan and Lahey, 2009, p. 17). Information flow here is characterized by messages that I send being more likely to be a function of what I deem others need to hear to best further the agenda or mission of my design. The self-authoring mind creates a filter for what it will allow to come through. It places a priority on receiving the information it has sought (Kegan and Lahey, 2009).

> The self-transforming mind also has a filter, but is not fused with it. The self-transforming mind can stand back from its own filter and look *at* it, not just *through* it. Therefore, when communicating, people with a self-transforming mind are not only advancing their agenda and design, they are also making space for the modification or expansion of their agenda or design (Kegan & Lahey, 2009, pp16-20).

These three stages are illustrated in Figure 4 along with the percentage distribution of these levels among adults.

Figure 4. Stages of Mental Complexity*

* Percentage distributions come from R. Kegan (1994) and W. Torbert (1987).

The need for a self-transforming mind certainly applies to those who aspire to be successful global leaders in today's complex business environment (Rhinesmith, 1996).

The vertical development part of the HV Model is a way to help leaders achieve Kegan and Lahey's Level 5 self-transforming mind by overcoming an "immunity to change." This is done through applying a vertical development process to the nine competencies. Experienced or emerging global leaders often feel comfortable in their current leadership style, and it may be difficult for them to change and fully perform these new competencies. They have developed an *immunity* to break out of their style and try new behaviors. They may be operating at levels lower than the self-transforming mind (either the socialized mind or the self-authoring mind).

Following the process described by Kegan and Lahey (2009), in this Chapter we present sample Behavior Change Maps for each of the nine competencies. We begin with a Behavior Change Map for the PATIENCE competency.

Patience Competency Development

A Behavior Change Map for **PATIENCE** is shown in figure 5:

Figure 5: <u>PATIENCE</u>
Behavior Change Map*

The ability to show patience in working with people of other cultures is difficult in the fast-paced global business environment. Being patient with people who speak a different primary language or have a different sense of time is the key here. "Go slow to go fast."

1 Behavior Goals (Visible Commitments)	2 Doing/Not Doing Instead (Behaviors Which Work Against the Goal)	3 Hidden Commitments That Compete with the Goals	4 My Big Assumptions Standing in the Way of Goal Achievement
I need to be more patient with people: • Wait till they have finished talking. • Talk slower. • Walk around the office slower. • Not pressure people so much. • Give other people a chance to talk. • Listen to people. **I need to be more patient in frustrating situations:** • Do not react immediately to the situation. • Try to understand why your expectation was not met. • Think of alternatives to get results: Allow more time, Ask for explanation, Modify your approach • Identify a person in your life who demonstrates a great deal of patience. Observe what that person does and try to do those things yourself. **Add your own actions.**	• I interrupt people when they are talking to me. • I make decisions very quickly. • I walk very fast around the office. • I talk very fast and very loud. • I sometimes forget to say hello to people. • I sometimes pay no attention to people who are talking. **Add your own:**	• Being fast and impatient to get results. • Not wasting my time on nonsense. • Not damaging my home life. • Not seeing my performance drop because of people wasting my time. • Not having my image and career stalled because my performance drops. **Add your own:**	• I will have to spend several more hours every day. It will mean long days. • My family will be affected. • My home life will affect my work life. • My attention will be diverted to nonsense things and that will delay important things. **Add your own:**

*Adapted from Petrie (2011 p. 33)

13

The Patience Competency Behavior Change Map is Interpreted in the Following Way:

- The first column is a set of behavior goals or new visual commitments.

- The second column is a possible set of current behaviors that work against the goals.

- The third column contains hidden commitments that compete with the goals.

- The fourth column lists some assumptions that underlie perceived difficulty in achieving the goals.

The development challenge for the Patience competency (Figure 5) is to reduce the column 2 behaviors and learn to engage in the column 1 behaviors. Looking at columns 2, 3 and 4, it can be seen that this person has built up a self-reinforcing system for the column 2 style. This person is in a hurry (and looks like it) makes decisions quickly and does not pay attention to others. This style fits his commitments to not waste time and to get results, which in turn supports his big assumptions in column 4. If this person is operating at the level of the self-authoring mind, it is extremely difficult to transition to the Level 5 self-transforming mind, which is necessary to engage in the column 1 behaviors. It may be that this leader, like many global leaders, operates at the self-authoring level, where they have advanced and been rewarded by strongly influencing others to follow their directions, plans and designs. This self-reinforcing system has worked well for this. However, by coming face to face with his assumptions, competing commitments, and current behavioral style, he may be able to break out of this style, advance to the Level 5 self-transforming mind and engage in column 1 behaviors. This is the big difference between levels of complexity— remaining at the self-authoring level will not allow the difficult process of change required in this example.

The coaching process in our HV Model is directed at buying in to the Behavior Change Map, which suggests a series of small experiments in the workplace to test out goal achievement and the validity of the assumptions. For example, this person could commit to talking slower and improve attention and listening skills by seeking verification of messages through paraphrasing. As these new behaviors settle in, he checks to see if his performance is really dropping or improving and if his assumptions are valid (maybe he has been overlooking "nonsense things").

APPLICATION CASE FOR PATIENCE

A French executive was transferred to the US to lead a multi-billion dollar division of his company. He was highly competent in the company technology, but he also brought with him his French style of leadership and management, which is called "demarche." This is a process of having the right intellectual approach to a problem, involving a lot of back and forth questioning of the nature and scope of the problem itself and requires consideration of all aspects and ramifications of potential solutions (Asselin & Mastron, 2001). His team was used to the American style, which is more data driven and more quickly reaches decisions and conclusions. His team felt that this executive was wasting a lot of time, not moving forward quickly enough in a very competitive market. His low score on the Patience scale and behavioral interview showed that he was exhibiting the behaviors in column 2. He could not understand why his team did not follow his style and his impatience was very pronounced in dealing with them. Working through his Behavior Change Map, he took very seriously experimenting with the Patience goals, as well as trying to achieve an "intercultural synergy" in this French/American style. Once his team noticed his new style and came to understand what he was trying to do, they put equal energy into becoming a better team than before.

Open-mindedness Competency Development

A Behavior Change Map for **OPEN-MINDEDNESS** is shown in Figure 6.

Figure 6: OPEN-MINDEDNESS
Behavior Change Map

The global business environment severely tests one's mind set. Being open to different values, beliefs and ways of thinking and doing things is essential for successful global leadership.

1 Behavior Goals (Visible Commitments)	2 Doing/Not Doing Instead (Behaviors Which Work Against the Goal)	3 Hidden Commitments That Compete with the Goals	4 My Big Assumptions Standing in the Way of Goal Achievement
I need to be more open-minded regarding other beliefs and ways of thinking and doing: • Challenge my own culture-based assumptions about others. • Withhold judgment and action until I get all relevant information. • Show respect, both verbally and in my body language. • Do not attempt to convince others of my spiritual and political beliefs. **Add your own actions:**	• I make judgments and act too quickly based on my own assumptions. • I get into lively discussions in which I press my spiritual or political beliefs. • I am not sure that I communicate and show respect for others (especially those who are different from me). **Add your own actions:**	• I need to stand up for my culture. • I need to explain and defend my spiritual or political beliefs. • I need to be seen as a leader with strong values and opinions. **Add your own actions:**	• I will have to compromise my values. • I will not be true to my spiritual or political beliefs. • I will be seen as weak and not standing for anything. **Add your own actions:**

We now have a Behavior Change Map for the Open-Mindedness competency. With coaching support, the Map is customized by each individual as they add to each column. This allows for vertical development and the opportunity for an individual to own their own development. As Petrie states, "people's motivations to grow are highest when they feel a sense of autonomy over their own development."

Again, as with the process for the Patience competency, the development challenge for this competency is to reduce the column 2 behaviors and learn to engage in the column 1 behaviors. Looking at columns 2, 3 and 4, it can be seen that this person has built up a self-reinforcing system for the column 2 style. This person is stuck in Bennett's Ethnocentric Defense Stage (Bennett, 1993). This style is based on very deep cultural, spiritual and political values, has apparently worked well for this person (or so he thinks) and is therefore very difficult to change. However, change toward a Level 5 self-transforming mind is possible through an understanding of the importance of this competency in leading across cultures, uncovering hidden commitments and assumptions and challenging these in small behavioral steps.

APPLICATION CASE FOR OPEN-MINDEDNESS

A young Italian plant manager was given an assignment at a plant in Turkey. He was single and very motivated to prove himself and excel at the company he worked for. He had a great deal of expertise related to the technical aspects of his job, but very limited people management skills.

Prior to the assignment, he completed an intercultural assessment along with a behavioral interview to validate the assessment and better understand his strengths and key areas for development. His scores on the assessment were below the norm in the area of Open-Mindedness. Then during the interview, these scores were validated. One example that he provided described how during one of his first trips outside of his home country, to Egypt, he saw a woman wearing a hijab or head wrap. His first reaction was to take a picture of her.

As he began to take the picture, her husband and family as well as other people nearby yelled at him and tried to take his camera away. His initial reaction was surprise and inability to comprehend what he had done wrong. At some point during the confrontation he realized that he had offended her and her family and apologized. The overall assessment found that he had a tendency to be nationalistic about his home country and judgmental or quick to judge what he viewed through his own cultural lens. He had very limited experience outside of his home country and also very strong feelings about the religion he was surrounded by as he was raised.

Experiences like this combined with a quality assessment and feedback session led him to be motivated to work toward development and growth in the area Open-Mindedness via a Behavior Change Map. He began by setting some visible behavior goals like learning as much as possible about a new environment prior to experiencing it and to not take even small actions like taking a picture in a different country for granted. Then he reviewed the behaviors he engaged in that worked against his goal of becoming more open-minded. For example he set a goal to consciously notice when he was making a judgement and then look at whether he was making that judgement based on his own assumptions and historical bias. Then he looked at his potential hidden commitments that compete for his ability to become more open-minded like nationalistic feelings about Italy or even a need based on his upbringing to defend his own spiritual beliefs.

Finally, he tried to consider his big assumptions. In his case, there was an unfounded assumption that somehow accepting other people's beliefs made him less committed to his own beliefs or that he would be perceived that way by his family.

As he progressed further and began his assignment, these new filters and goals formed a new canvass for his experience. He began to learn more about the culture and became friends with some local nationals. Overall, with support and as he gave attention to his development plan, he made great strides toward his goal of becoming more open minded. He was encouraged to reflect on his initial goals and later experiences after he was in country for two months and then again at the end of his assignment. The richness of this process for him became a solid positive benchmark as he continued forward with a successful career.

Even Disposition Competency Development

A behavior change map for the **EVEN DISPOSITION** competency is shown in Figure 7. A leader who scores below the norm on this scale is likely demonstrating the column 2 behaviors, which he or she may not be conscious of. Focused on high standards and not making mistakes, this leader is hindering high performance team function by showing frustration and not helping the team to work through difficult situations.

Figure 7. EVEN DISPOSITION
Behavior Change Map

Successful global leaders have the ability to maintain an even disposition under a variety of conditions. In difficult or confusing situations they are able to remain calm, exhibit a good sense of humor and allow for mistakes in themselves and others.

1 Behavior Goals (Visible Commitments)	2 Doing/Not Doing Instead (Behaviors Which Work Against the Goal)	3 Hidden Commitments That Compete with the Goals	4 My Big Assumptions Standing in the Way of Goal Achievement
I need to display a calm demeanor during difficult or stressful situations. I can do this by: • Recognizing when I am feeling anxiety or frustration and learn and apply various relaxation techniques prior to taking action. **I need to enjoy and utilize humor during stressful situations. I can do this by:** • Enjoying and laughing when others bring humor into stressful situations. • Bring humor into difficult situations and lighten the mood for my team. • Smiling more. **I need to create an environment where mistakes are allowed. I can do this by:** • Admitting my own mistakes with a sense of humor and not overreacting. **Add your own actions:**	• When things go wrong I can overreact. • I can get frustrated when others use humor during times of great stress. • I am very hard on myself and get angry when I make a mistake. • My work demeanor is very serious and I intend for it to be that way. • I don't use or enjoy humor very often. **Add your own:**	• Utilizing a relaxation method will distract me from addressing the problem at hand. • If I smile or enjoy humor people will think I am not very serious about my work and therefore won't take me seriously. • I don't react to humor because I often do not understanding the joke or what people are laughing about. • I hold myself to a very high standard and don't allow myself to make mistakes so that others won't find fault in me. **Add your own:**	• If I make a mistake people won't respect my authority. • If I allow for people to make mistakes, people will think it is acceptable to make mistakes. • If I react quickly the problem will be resolved more quickly. • Anxiety management techniques don't work. • Laughter or humor has no place in the work environment. **Add your own:**

20

APPLICATION CASE FOR EVEN DISPOSITION

A European executive was surprised to see his score below the norm on the Even Disposition competency. He had always assumed that his leadership style, focused on technology and process, was successful and appreciated by his executive team. Following his GLTAP feedback and development session and working through his Behavior Change Map, he discussed his style with his team. They were reluctant to explain how his outward disposition had negatively affected team effectiveness, given his outstanding capabilities in the important technologies of the company. Upon assuring his team that he really was concerned about how he appeared to them in critical times of urgency, they explained that he did "loose his cool." This information confirmed to him that he needed to develop and transform his style (transitioning from Column 2 behaviors to the Column 1 Goals) and he was on the road to becoming a more effective leader.

Lifetime Learning Competency Development

A Behavior Change Map for the **LIFETIME LEARNING** competency is shown in Figure 8. A leader who scores below the norm on this GLTAP scale is entirely focused on what she considers her company's business, and she has not developed a commitment to learning beyond this. She does not realize the importance to her role as a global leader of acquiring and maintaining a broad understand of what is going on in the world. She seems to have an issue with work/life balance, but her development challenge is to devote more time at least to world issues that affect her business.

Figure 8. <u>LIFETIME LEARNING</u>
Behavioral Change Map

A deep knowledge of other nations and cultures is one of the factors that differentiates successful global leaders from unsuccessful ones. The ability to gain this knowledge is characteristic of those who are committed to a pattern of lifetime learning. This means being interested in and conversant about the history and traditions of other cultures as well as current events.

1 Behavior Goals (Visible Commitments)	2 Doing/Not Doing Instead (Behaviors Which Work Against the Goal)	3 Hidden Commitments That Compete with the Goals	4 My Big Assumptions Standing in the Way of Goal Achievement
I need to actively seek information about people's cultures, local issues and global news from a wide variety of sources. I can to this by: • Identifying a minimum of three separate news sources (possibly the internet, newspapers and colleagues). • Make a habit of setting aside time daily and weekly to seek out and be informed by these sources. **Add your own actions:**	• I am too focused on staying on top of work and day to day tasks to read non-work related things or pay attention to the news. • I get my news and information about local events from my spouse or partner so I don't need to take the time to do it myself. • I actively seek out and stay informed about the news but only from one news source. • During my free time I don't want to spend time doing research and watching the news. **Add your own:**	• Reading or listening to the news will take too much time away from the work at hand. • I don't enjoy the news or I find it boring. • I am too busy to take time to stay up on current events. • I don't have time to talk to colleagues about things that aren't specifically work related. **Add your own:**	• The news and world events have no direct effect on my life. • I don't have the ability to affect change on anything I see in the news so why concern myself with it? • I am not aware of how cultural differences can affect interactions and of how much information is available to me about these differences. **Add your own:**

APPLICATION CASE FOR LIFETIME LEARNING

An American female engineer was promoted to a leadership role and assigned to a team working in India. While she had travelled internationally, she had never lived internationally prior to this assignment. Historically, she had not been interested in global news or the nuances of different cultures. It was just something she didn't have time for. In India she became very focused on the project details and the technology they were developing. She was very knowledgeable about the work they were conducting and she worked long hours. Over time, she found that a key colleague and subordinate on the project who was a male Indian national was very resistant to her leadership. Day after day he seemed to be more difficult to work with. She became so frustrated that she was considering returning home early and taking on a new position back home.

Several months into her assignment, she attended a company-wide global leadership training program where she completed the GLTAP Assessment and worked with a certified coach. Through this process she became aware of how she needed to learn more about the culture of India. Also, she received feedback about how she appeared to others. They reported that she was so focused on the technology and concept she was working on that she did not adjust to the Indian workplace culture. Working with her coach, she developed a plan that involved change mapping new approaches to her work environment. Over the next several weeks she sought her Indian colleague out and asked him for his input and found ways to show respect for his insight. This effort took time, but eventually, they developed a much improved working relationship. Also, the time she took to learn more about Indian culture deeply improved her overall adjustment and enjoyment of the assignment in India.

Navigating Ambiguity Competency Development

A Behavior Change Map for the **NAVIGATING AMBIGUITY** competency is presented in Figure 9. The leader described in Column 2 is most comfortable with known challenges and solutions. He may be operating at the stage of the Self-Authoring Mind, where his communication is characterized by what "he deems others need to hear to best further the agenda of his own design." In order to achieve the Self-Transforming stage, he needs to challenge himself with problems and situations that are unfamiliar to him and to see things as others do in order to expand his agenda. He might be applying known solutions to the incredibly ambiguous, culturally confusing world of global business and therefore missing opportunities.

Figure 9. NAVIGATING AMBIGUITY

Behavioral Change Map

Global leaders with a high tolerance for ambiguity can generally experience and manage uncertain situations easily, while leaders with a lower tolerance for ambiguity might handle those same situations with difficulty and emotional discomfort.

1 Behavior Goals (Visible Commitments)	2 Doing/Not Doing Instead (Behaviors Which Work Against the Goal)	3 Hidden Commitments That Compete with the Goals	4 My Big Assumptions Standing in the Way of Goal Achievement
I need to become more comfortable with uncertainty and the unfamiliar. I can to this by: • Notice if I am seeing something through my own cultural lens and try to view it through the lens of another culture. • Recognize that the situation might not lend itself to categorization, planning or organization. It may just need to exist until further study or progress is made. **I need to be able to plan and take appropriate action in the face of ambiguity.** • Reflect how I managed previous ambiguous times, research, ask for input, look for alternatives, execute and allow for mistakes. **Add your own actions:**	• My first reaction is to reject or judge the unusual or different. • I try to package, categorize and plan myself out of ambiguity. • I push to find certainty. • I want to understand the whole situation and find a solution fast and this closure can sometimes be premature. • I may hang on to a solution or method too long because I am familiar with it. • I am staying safe. **Add your own:**	• People expect me to understand, know the right answer, and act immediately. • I am not allowed to make mistakes. **Add your own:**	• I am expected to grasp situations quickly. • I must maintain control in most situations. • I cannot appear uncomfortable with things that exist outside of my normal experiences. • Every problem is solvable and certainty and clarity can be found if I look hard enough. **Add your own:**

25

APPLICATION CASE FOR NAVIGATING AMBIGUITY

An Italian male Engineer relocated with his wife to Kuwait. While they had done their research about living in a country that had a very different lifestyle and culture, he very quickly became uncomfortable and anxious because virtually everything from the weather, environment, style of dress, religious practices, food and more was new to him. Some days he felt virtually frozen and unable to move forward to do simple tasks. Over time, and with the help of his wife and supportive colleagues, he became more familiar with his new environment. He felt that his time in Kuwait was a positive experience overall, however, in some ways he felt that he had just "survived" the assignment instead of embracing and enjoying it.

This Engineer had great difficulty with ambiguity. His academic area had contributed to his mindset of structure and order, so that dealing with the ambiguities of life and work in Kuwait were particularly difficult for him. People who struggle with ambiguity like this engineer say that they can feel stuck or frozen when faced with the unknown. While it was difficult for him, it was also a great opportunity for him to develop his ability to navigate ambiguity. It is likely that he and his wife would have benefitted from more support prior to their assignment to identify areas where they might have difficulty along with creating a plan for them as they were adjusting to life in Kuwait.

His next assignment was for a position in Mexico. His Change Map for Ambiguity provided him with deep insight into this developmental area and helped him to create a thorough plan for building on his experiences in Kuwait and adapting to the Ambiguities of life and work in Mexico.

Locus of Control Competency Development

A Behavior Change Map for the **LOCUS OF CONTROL** competency appears in Figure 10. A leader who scores below the norm on this scale has an external locus of control, believing that much of her world is and has been beyond her control. This has led to a lack of taking the initiative in situations that she perceives as beyond her capabilities to manage. The challenge for her is to engage in incremental "experiments" in the workplace to test out the taking of control and initiative and thus to disprove the assumptions that have led to her external locus and lack of initiative.

Figure 10. LOCUS OF CONTROL

Behavioral Change Map

J.B. Rotter's Locus of Control is one of the most well researched psychological concepts (Rutter, 1966). This is defined as the extent to which individuals believe that they can take the initiative and control events affecting them. Individuals who have an internal locus of control believe that the events in their lives are generally the result of their own behavior and actions, and they take responsibility for them. On the other hand, individuals who have an external locus of control believe that the events in their lives are generally determined by chance, fate, or other people, and they direct responsibility elsewhere.

1 Behavior Goals (Visible Commitments)	2 Doing/Not Doing Instead (Behaviors Which Work Against the Goal)	3 Hidden Commitments That Compete with the Goals	4 My Big Assumptions Standing in the Way of Goal Achievement
I need to develop more of a belief that I can influence situations in my life (including undue pressure from others): • Approach things that are important to me with a belief that I can control the situation. • Show personal responsibility for my decisions and actions. • Take more initiative to get things done. • Speak up and take more of a lead in meetings. Add your own actions:	• Being in the right place at the right time has worked well for me, so I haven't had to expend a lot of energy to control events. • I usually go along with what others want. • I wait to hear from others before I say much of anything. Add your own:	• I don't want to be seen as too aggressive or controlling. • I shouldn't have to take responsibility for things that are really beyond my control. Add your own:	• No matter what I have tried to do, events seemed to just run their own course. • It is better to go along with others than to try to lead in a different direction. • I might be seen as impulsive and shallow if I speak up too soon. Add your own:

A female financial executive from the United States was selected for an assignment in China. She completed the GLTAP Assessment and received coaching and feedback support as well. During her process, she and her coach agreed that she had an external Locus of Control. Her style was often to sit back and observe situations prior to taking action and speaking up. Also, she did not like confrontation. This was a complex developmental opportunity when looking at a new leadership role in China, especially as a female leader. On one hand, her ability to be patient and listen before taking action was a positive asset in a leader, but there were many things she could do to strengthen leadership potential in China.

Together, she and her coach worked through the HV Model and Change Mapping process. She set some behavior goals like ensuring that she was taking the lead when necessary in meetings or on projects (and it is necessary to do this much more often in China in order to be perceived as an effective leader). In the past, she often felt like accurate numbers speak for themselves and give obvious direction toward future actions, but she began to see that this was not enough and that she needed to take on the role of a leader in framing the goals of her team. A strong leader needs to be comfortable with confrontation, but she believed that it was important to not be seen as too aggressive or controlling. This is a hidden/competing commitment that she had been holding on to for a long time. Overall she determined to more consciously recognize how her own efforts and actions can dictate the direction of her team and the outcomes she desires in her own life. Going into this new challenge, she felt more confidence due to this analysis and preparation.

Demonstrating Creativity Competency Development

A behavior change map for the **DEMONSTRATING CREATIVITY** competency is presented in Figure 11.

The development challenge here is for a leader to go beyond approaches and solutions that are familiar and tested. This requires dealing with risk and seeking input from team members with divergent thinking. Global business sometimes moves at high speed, so it may seem counter –intuitive to take the time to come up with creative approaches, but new ideas can result in big wins.

Complexity is perhaps the most compelling issue faced by global leaders. Developing creativity in leadership style can meet this challenge by helping to see around corners, predict outcomes and act despite uncertainty. Successful global leadership is also about influencing others, finding ways to select, retain and motivate diverse talent.

Figure 11. DEMONSTRATING CREATIVITY

Behavioral Change Map

While it may be true that some people seem to be more creative than others, it is possible for everyone to become more creative in their approaches to leadership challenges. This involves a commitment to divergent thinking, as compared to a convergent process.

1 Behavior Goals (Visible Commitments)	2 Doing/Not Doing Instead (Behaviors Which Work Against the Goal)	3 Hidden Commitments That Compete with the Goals	4 My Big Assumptions Standing in the Way of Goal Achievement
I need to be more creative in how I approach problems and deal with people. • Try different and unfamiliar ways of doing things, even if they are unconventional. • Look forward to challenges. • Develop a set of alternatives (including some unusual ones) for decisions and solutions. • Seek out and mix with different kinds of people. • Come up with ways to form teams that maximize diversity. • Get the best thinking from team members by asking open-ended, high value questions. • Reward innovation in approaches and solutions among your teams. **Add your own actions:**	• I look for and am most comfortable with things that are predictable and familiar. • I take on more of the same types of things that I am used to. • I decide on one best approach early, without taking the time to consider others. • I am most comfortable with people who are like me. **Add your own:**	• I have never considered myself to be very creative. • It takes too much time and effort to come up with new ways of doing things when tried and true works just fine. **Add your own:**	• Getting better and better at what I do and the ways that I do things is more productive than trying new things. • Going too far with innovation is just too risky. • People who are more alike work best as a team. **Add your own:**

31

APPLICATION CASE FOR DEMONSTRATING CREATIVITY

In their book "Immunity to Change" Kegan and Lahey (2009 pages 32-36), describe Peter, a CEO of a large financial services company. His continued success was hindered by his "hidden, competing commitments," which, among other things was "to preserve my sense of myself as the super problem solver, the one who knows best, the one who is in control—yesterday, today and tomorrow." These commitments were blocking him from his goals of "being receptive to new ideas" and being more flexible and open."

This case is reminiscent of our research of 1880 global leaders, reported in Chapter 5, where our competency of Demonstrating Creativity was one of the factors that significantly predicted separate criteria of success over time. We would therefore assume that Peter would score below the norm on this GLTAP competency. We would add to his Map creativity goals of trying different ways of doing things, taking the time to develop alternative solutions, getting the best from diverse team members and rewarding creativity among them. These goals can be achieved by facing what Peter is doing now to limit creativity (deciding on one best approach early, without taking the time to consider others) and by challenging assumptions like getting better at what he does and the ways that he does things is more productive than trying new things.

Adapting Socially Competency Development

A Behavior Change Map for **ADAPTING SOCIALLY** appears in Figure 12.

Leaders who are lacking in social skills are limited in what they can accomplish in the global business environment. Building positive relationships across cultures is often the key to success in many countries. The challenge here is to realize that building these relationships IS part of the leadership role. This involves showing genuine interest in other individuals and getting comfortable in social situations.

Figure 12. ADAPTING SOCIALLY

Behavioral Change Map

A major aspect of global leadership success is influencing people and working with individuals and teams to achieve business goals. This requires the ability to show interest in others and to engage in social activities that bind people together.

1 Behavior Goals (Visible Commitments)	2 Doing/Not Doing Instead (Behaviors Which Work Against the Goal)	3 Hidden Commitments That Compete with the Goals	4 My Big Assumptions Standing in the Way of Goal Achievement
I need to engage with and become more comfortable with people in social situations and to show others that I am interested in them. • Seek out and participate in social activities, even if they interfere with my personal time. • Let others know who I am – not be difficult to get to know. • Learn things about people I meet and remember them in future discussions (including the correct pronunciation of names and titles!) • Genuinely enjoy and get energized by discussions in social situations. **Add your own actions:**	• I am uncomfortable in social situations. • I can't seem to remember names of people I meet. • I get nervous when I meet new people. • I like to be alone and do things by myself. **Add your own:**	• Work life and social life are different and separate. • Spending social time with others compromises my leadership authority. • Learning personal information about others is not part of my role and will negatively influence my decisions. **Add your own:**	• It is important to maintain a certain distance between me and those who work for me. **Add your own:**

33

An American project team leader was working on a promising proposal for a large project in Spain that involved a Spanish company being considered as a partner. The head of the Spanish company had been in the US with his team several times and the American leader had been in Spain with his team. The American had not taken much time to spend with the Spanish in either country because of what he perceived to be schedule and task priorities. The Spanish leader had invited him to dinner in Spain, but the American had just not been able to find the time.

The project involved the selection of a Spanish sub-contractor for a critical component of the project. The American and two of his team members traveled to Spain to work with the Spanish company to select this sub-contractor. They brought with them their company's procedure for competitive selection of sub-contractors.

Again, the Spanish leader invited the Americans to a social function, but they declined. When the Americans met with the Spanish team it became apparent that they had a very different approach. The Spanish leader said "I would like to use a company that I have worked with for a long time. I have a good relationship with the head of the company, who is my cousin, and I know that he will do a good job." The American leader explained how important it was to get the best sub-contractor at the lowest price. "Our company's competitive bid approach will allow us to look at several companies and pick the one that best meets our needs at the lowest cost." The Spanish leader said he already knew the other companies and assured the Americans that his cousin's company was the best. The American leader at one point in the discussions appeared upset and frustrated, saying "The only way forward here is to use our competitive bid process. We will show you how it works."

After several more meetings, it was clear that the Spanish company was just not going to use the American competitive bid process. The

Americans returned to the US, feeling very uneasy about the Spanish company and concerned about their chances for winning the project.

They later learned that a competitive consortium had won the bid for the project.

This case illustrates the importance of Adapting Socially to global business success. The American project leader was doing his best to win the project, but he did not understand the importance of relationships in the Spanish business culture and did not have the social skills required. Had he taken the time and opportunities to develop a relationship with the Spanish leader, they might together have come up with a solution that they both could agree on. For example, they could together audit the cousin's company to see if it was a good choice. The cousin would have a great deal on the line (he and his company would lose great "face" in the relationship based Spanish business culture). He would not go forward if he wasn't certain of good performance.

Had the American engaged in the GLTAP/Behavior Change process, he might have developed the social skills required to perform in this critical situation.

(Note: Spain is ranked 30th out of 178 on the Transparency International Corruption Index, number 1 being the least corrupt and 159 the most. Spain's corruption index is 6.2 on a 10 point scale, with 10 being the least corrupt. The U.S. ranks 22nd, with an index of 7.1).

Instilling Trust Competency Development

A final Behavior Change Map for **INSTILLING TRUST** is presented in Figure 13.

Steven M. R. Covey has made a powerful case that low levels of trust slow down everything—every decision, every communication, and every relationship (Covey, 2006). On the other hand, high trust produces SPEED, which is critical in the global business environment. Leaders who do not trust easily need to first develop this competency in behavioral style by following the behavioral goals in column 1. They then must learn what trust means to the people in the countries of operation and work to instill trust in their business relationships.

Figure 13. <u>INSTILLING TRUST</u>

Behavioral Change Map

The ability to instill trust in the organization and among teams that they lead is a hallmark of successful global leaders. Being trusted and trusting employees and involving them in the decision-making process results in better overall decisions, greater acceptance of these decisions and increased satisfaction.

1 Behavior Goals (Visible Commitments)	2 Doing/Not Doing Instead (Behaviors Which Work Against the Goal)	3 Hidden Commitments That Compete with the Goals	4 My Big Assumptions Standing in the Way of Goal Achievement
I need to develop my competency for instilling trust in my relationships and in my organization culture: • Learn what trust means in the cultures with which I work, compared to my own, and demonstrate those trusting behaviors. • Carefully communicate my expectations up-front, understand the expectations of others, and make sure that these expectations are compatible. • Listen to others first, before communicating my agenda. • Create transparency so that others do not feel that I am hiding anything and I do not spring surprises on them. • Practice accountability by doing what I say I will do and take accountability for my actions. **Add your own actions:**	• I just go forward without paying much attention to instilling trust. • I don't trust easily and I usually look for things that others do that shows that I can't trust them. • People too often do not follow through with what I expect of them. **Add your own:**	• As a strong leader, others know that they can trust me—it goes with my position. • At my level, there are many things that must remain hidden from others. **Add your own:**	• Trust pretty much means the same thing all over the world. • I will be disappointed and compromised when I trust too early and too easily. • Others will take advantage of me. **Add your own:**

37

APPLICATION CASE INSTILLING TRUST

A young British manager was placed as the team leader for his company's new global product initiative. Much of the work was virtual, since the multicultural team was working from their home countries—the U.S., Costa Rica, Japan and Malaysia. The British team leader was considered highly skilled in the product being developed. He had convened an initial face-to-face meeting, and then proceeded to work with the team on a virtual basis. It became apparent that the project was going to take much more time and effort than anticipated, and they became under great pressure to move forward. The team leader could not get the team "on the same page." The major problem seemed to be that there just wasn't much trust among team members, beginning with the team leader.

The team leader took the opportunity to complete the GLTAP, and sure enough, he scored below the norm on the Trust Competency. He had an "immunity to change" process embedded in his style, where he was having difficulty instilling trust because he was committed to his belief that trust went along with his leadership position. He was also committed that some things needed to remain hidden from the team. His assumptions were that trust meant the same things all over the world and that others would take advantage of him if he trusted too easily.

These insights allowed him to not spend all of his time on the product tasks, but to devote energy into building a culture of trust among the team (which was difficult, because it required him to break his circular immunity to change by going against his commitments and assumptions). He learned that the Costa Ricans linked trust to building relationships; that the Japanese linked it to having sufficient information because of their high need for certainty, and the differences between the US/Britain and Malaysia on Power Distance (the US and Britain are comfortable with a small distance between the leader and the team, but the Malaysians prefer a large distance.

In discussing these differences with the team, they were able to create a "synergy" in their team style, accommodating each culture. The team leader also worked to make his expectations more clear, listening to the team before making decisions, being more transparent, and practicing accountability himself. The team was able to move forward, complete the new product and help get it to their market.

This application of Instilling Trust concludes our Vertical Development chapter. We now turn to an even deeper approach to development by addressing a Growth Mindset and Managing Transitions.

CHAPTER 4

Developing a Growth Mindset
and Managing Transitions

Resistance to Change

In her book, <u>Mindset</u>, Dr. Carol Dweck (2006) states that "our best bet is not simply to hire the most talented managers we can find and turn them loose, but to look for managers who also embody a growth mindset: a zest for teaching and learning, an openness to giving and receiving feedback, and an ability to confront and surmount obstacles." While many people respond well to the process of feedback and "making the connection" to recognize their strengths and developmental opportunities and become motivated for personal growth and change, some people don't. In some cases, if a company finds that an individual has some areas for development but is resistant to change, they may decide to choose a different candidate for the international leadership role. However, for many reasons, they sometimes must select a candidate even if their selection is resistant to change and feedback.

These people may have a "fixed versus growth" mindset (Dweck, 2006). We have found that in some cases individuals do not accept feedback or, they do acknowledge the feedback and "see themselves in their scores," but assume that their scores are a permanent part of who they are and therefore unchangeable.

Dweck explains that "the exciting part is that the growth mindset can be taught." Our HV Model works toward an initial path of recognition and feedback based on a behavioral interview and then toward customized change mapping toward targeted growth. In order to encourage a growth mindset as a framework for development in the GLTAP competencies, the coaches certified to administer the GLTAP and use the HV Model aspire to put the individual in a growth mindset during feedback by presenting the competencies as learnable and giving feedback in a "way that promotes learning and future success" (Dweck, 2006).

Managing Transitions

As a final step in our HV Model process of global leadership development, we have incorporated William Bridges' Managing Transitions process (Bridges, 1991). In his words "the process helps to understand the difficulties faced whenever you try to get people to change the way they do things---the blank stares, muttering, foot-dragging, and subtle sabotage that turns a good plan into an unworkable mess."

As the transition is made from current behavior (column 2) to behavioral goals (column 1) in each of the Behavior Change Maps, Bridges' process can be applied as illustrated in Figure 14.

Figure 14. Managing Transitions*

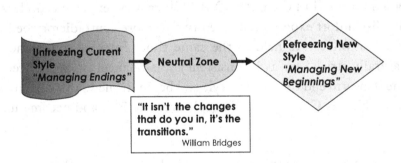

Based on the work of William Bridges "Managing Transitions" (1991)

Managing Endings

New behavioral goals cannot just begin to be performed. Current behavior must first be ENDED. This is the unfreezing stage first described by Kurt Lewin (1947). As attempts are made to end current style, it may feel uncomfortable because doing this in a certain way has become a familiar pattern. For example, in trying to become more patient, a familiar pattern may be making decisions quickly, speaking rapidly, and getting frustrated when expectations are not met. This style can END by being MINDFUL and---

- Taking more time to make decisions.

- Speaking slower and more clearly.

- Breathing deeply and trying to remain calm during frustrating times.

Neutral Zone

As progress is made through the transition process, the NEUTRAL ZONE will be entered, which involves ending current style and trying out the new one. The feeling of dis-orientation and what is called COGNITIVE DISSONANCE may be experienced. This is the discomfort experienced when two or more contradictory beliefs, ideas or values are held at the same time. Internal consistency is naturally strived for as inconsistency (dissonance) is experienced as one strives to end the current style and begin the new. This dissonance is resolved as Column 1 style goals are practiced and become more natural.

The good news about this neutral zone is the opportunity that it presents for innovation and creativity. As current style is unfrozen, and the experience of being "between trapezes," the mind opens up to ways of doing things that had not been thought of before.

Managing New Beginnings

While working through the neutral zone and beginning to engage in the Column 1 goals as the new, preferred style, it may be seen that the Column 4 "Big Assumptions" were really not valid. The messy part comes from the start and stop process where one falls back occasionally to the old style. Getting positive feedback about the new style helps to keep it in place and reinforced. A new self-esteem and self-development may now actually seem to be rather fun!

The goal of this managing change and transition process is to enable people to be more effective global leaders, working successfully across cultures. Managing the NEW BEGINNINGS is the third and final step in this transition process.

CHAPTER 5

THE STUDIES:
Identifying the Key Competencies That Are Critical For Successful Global Leaders

One common, critical request that we receive from global businesses is "what are the key competencies required of successful global leaders?" They want to know what they should be looking for and how they can measure and identify it in their current and potential leaders. Only after we identify these competencies and know our targets for development can we work toward growth and positive change.

We have been working in this field for decades, utilizing well researched tools to identify key characteristics that lead to successful adjustment to living and working in different countries. However, based on demand from our clients, we felt there was a great need to conduct further review and research to identify the key competencies of successful global leaders.

To do this, we partnered with Right Management to conduct a study to summarize what has been done on this subject and to identify the competencies of global leaders (Tucker et al. 2014). A set of six competencies were produced, which predicted a set of separate leadership success criteria over time. Then, in order to identify a set of competencies that was larger and more useful for applied development, we conducted a second study to determine if we could expand on the original six competencies.

What follows are summaries of the two studies that form the Horizontal part of our HV Model.

STUDY ONE: Leading Across Cultures in the Human Age: An Empirical Investigation of Intercultural Competency Among Global Leaders (Tucker, et al. 2014)

The Need for Better Global Business Leaders

The emergence of globalization just a short time ago has become the norm. Companies adept at identifying business opportunities anywhere in the world and effectively deploying resources to capture those opportunities are enjoying unprecedented success. The days are gone when a major company can be complacent by being successful only in its home market, or even in one or two cross border markets. Even if a major company chooses not to expand globally, international competitors will enter its favorite markets. Among the challenges facing these companies are competing in a global environment and developing leadership talent.

To be successful, global organizations need leaders who can drive business on a global scale. We are now in the Human Age, where Talentism is the new Capitalism. This means that talent, not capital is the greatest need and key to success. Most global organizations today have little difficulty raising capital for their enterprises, given their high stock valuations and eager investors. But the war for talent goes on for those who can lead these enterprises. Winning this war requires talent strategies that focus on selecting, developing and nurturing global leaders.

Leading across cultures is a critical element of leading in the Human Age and unleashing the power of what is humanly possible. It often requires making decisions in complex or ambitious environments, understanding cultural nuances and adapting one's style accordingly. A good track record in one country does not guarantee success in the global arena, nor will merely exposing high-performing leaders to new cultures make them effective multinational leaders.

Recent studies by IBM of 1500 CEOs and DDI of 14,320 HR professionals and business leaders show that a majority of companies do not have the leaders needed to keep up with the speed of business, are not satisfied with the quality of their leaders (particularly Asian leaders), and do not have the bench strength to meet future business needs (IBM 2011; Boatman & Wellins 2011).

These two surveys are concerned with leadership in general. The situation with global leadership talent is even more dire. Researchers have argued that global leadership is more complex than domestic leadership in that leadership responsibilities and issues span across cultures (e.g., ethical challenges, team building, dealing with different perspectives) (Osland & Bird 2006). Very few companies, indeed, would say that they are satisfied with leaders' current proficiency in this type of leadership in their organizations.

There is a growing awareness that a new kind of leadership is emerging to show the way. Perhaps this was best stated by the Conference Board: "The pace of globalizing business strategy is staggering. Successful implementation of strategy, however, by interculturally competent people, supported by appropriate corporate practice, is the greatest need and the key to success." An article written by Joann S. Lublin in the Wall Street Journal stated: "Global businesses are looking for leaders who have the ability to move easily between different cultures... Finding such executives is very challenging... The talent pool is very small" (Lublin 2011, page B1). A study by Right Management and the Chally Group found that some 80% of HR professionals rated Cultural Assimilation as the greatest challenge facing successful leaders outside of their home country (Right Management 2011). A major study found that "Cultural issues will dominate the new competencies that will be required for global leaders over the next ten years" (Training Magazine 2011). Jim Collins, in his book Good to Great (Collins 2001) provided powerful support to the idea of people first. He found that the first step in taking a good company to a great one was not strategy, but "getting the right people on the bus, in the right seats, and then figuring out how to take the business someplace great." In the global business environment, the international bus must be led by people who can perform at high levels across cultures.

Research on Global Leadership

Although the field of global leadership research is new and emerging (Mendenhall et al. 2008) a number of studies have been reported in recent years. Summaries of these appear in Dickson, et al. (2003), House, et al. (1997), Dorfman (2003), Peterson and Hunt (1997), and Mendenhall et al. (2008). These studies, taken together, have included a large number of leadership competencies (perhaps over 50).

The early literature on global leadership historically focused on U.S. samples without carefully testing whether the research findings generalize across cultures outside the U.S. Over the past twenty years, researchers have started to test and validate theories and models of global leadership across cultures. This allows them to identify the capabilities needed for successful global leadership with more accuracy.

For example, Kuhlmann and Stahl (1998) studied expatriates to determine the competencies that predict their effectiveness (reported in Stahl 2001). They found that seven competencies are needed for global leaders to be successful including:

- Tolerance for ambiguity,
- Behavioral flexibility,
- Goal orientation,
- Sociability,
- Empathy,
- Non-judgmentalness, and
- Meta-communication skills.

House, et al. (2002) reported the results of their Global Leadership and Organizational Behavior Effectiveness (GLOBE) project, in which they studied leaders spanning 61 nations to find globally universal leadership competencies. They found support for nine global leadership competencies:

- Uncertainty avoidance (degree to which people rely on norms, rituals)

- Power distance (degree to which power is equally shared)

- Societal emphasis on collectivism (degree to which norms and practices reward collective distribution of resources)

- Family organizational collectivistic practices (degree to which individuals express pride, loyalty, and cohesiveness in families or orgs)

- Gender egalitarianism (degree to which gender role differences are minimized)

- Assertiveness (degree to which individuals are assertive in social relationships)

- Future orientation (degree to which individuals invest in the future)

- Performance orientation (degree to which people are rewarded for performance improvement/excellence)

- Humane orientation (degree to which people are rewarded for being friendly, caring, kind to others)

More recently, McCall and Hollenbeck (2002) found support for seven global competencies after they surveyed global leaders across 36 countries. They found support for the following competencies:

- Flexibility in strategy and tactics,
- Cultural sensitivity,
- Ability to deal with complexity,
- Resilience and resourcefulness,
- Honesty and integrity,

- Personal stability, and
- Sound technical skills.

This literature supports the need for several areas of investigation that are addressed in the present study:

- The need to study a representative sample comprised exclusively of global leaders.
- The need for a concise set of intercultural competencies and a separate set of global leadership success factors with good psychometric properties that can be used to compare among leaders of different nationalities.
- The need to validate intercultural competencies against separate criteria of global leadership success.
- The need to detect social desirability or "fake good" responses in self-response instruments and make appropriate corrections.

Questions Addressed in the Study

In order to meet these needs, the following questions were addressed in the study:

- What are the intercultural competencies among global leaders?
- What are the strongest of these competencies and those in need of greatest development?
- How do these competencies differ across nationalities?
- What are the areas of greatest leadership success?
- How do these success factors differ across nationalities?
- Which competencies are most strongly predictive of leadership success?

Leadership Theory

Leadership theory has focused on the traits of a leader, the attributes that a leader applies, and the situation in which leadership behavior occurs (see special issue in American Psychologist, Volume 62, Issue 1, 2007). Zaccaro (2007) offered the following trait-based model of effective leadership (Figure 15) wherein distal leader traits (distal attributes) affect proximal attributes, and together these attributes influence leader processes (moderated by operating environment), which in turn influences indicators of leader performance. Given that the field of global leadership remains in its infancy Bird, et al. (2008), the study reported here adopts this general trait-based model of leader effectiveness, applies it to global leadership effectiveness, and attempts to identify a more precise set of proximal attributes specifically relevant to global leadership. In addition, the present study attempts to establish an efficient set of global leader effectiveness criteria.

Fig. 15: Leader Performance Model

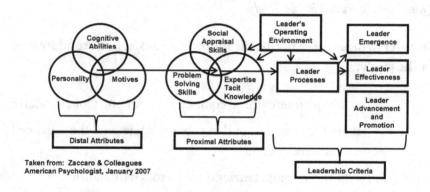

Intercultural Competence Theory and Model
Competency Standards

We agree with Bird (2008, p. 65) that "there are three clear standards that must be met to define an individual characteristic or capacity as a competency: (1) it must exist prior to performance; (2) it must be causally linked to performance; and (3) it must be possessed by superior, but not by average or subpar, performers." These standards guided our research method. We assessed competencies prior to assessing performance; we linked competencies to performance, and; we predicted membership in the top 20% of our leadership sample on performance factors.

Competency Definition and Theoretical Model

We agree with the definition of global leadership competencies as stated by Jokinen (2005) "those universal qualities that enable individuals to perform their job outside their own nationality as well as organizational culture, no matter what their educational or ethnic background is, what functional area their job description represents, or what organization they come from." As stated earlier, over 50 leadership competencies (Jokinen's "Universal Qualities") have been studied. As a starting point for our study, we began with the Tucker, et al. (2004) study in which 14 intercultural competencies were measured among 2131 corporate expatriates representing 11 nationalities (many of whom were leaders) and used these competencies to predict separate criteria of intercultural adjustment among 157 of these expatriates. Intercultural adjustment was in turn correlated with an expatriate job performance scale. The 2004 Tucker et al. study was based on a theoretical model that emerged over 30 years of empirical field research (Yellen and Mumford (1975); Tucker et al. (1978); Hawes and Kealey (1981); Tucker (1982); Tucker (1983); Tucker, (1994); The model provided a framework for defining and measuring intercultural adjustment among expatriates and predicting it from antecedent intercultural competencies. We examined this model for logical application to global leaders, modified and added to it based on the literature, and settled on a new model that we call Transcultural Leadership, which is illustrated in Figure 16 and then described.

Fig. 16 Transcultural Leadership Model

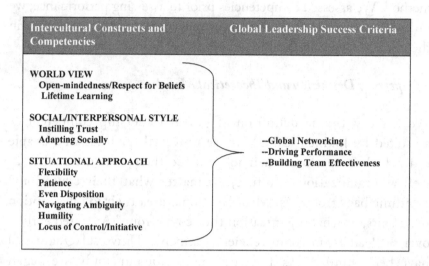

Intercultural Constructs and Competencies	Global Leadership Success Criteria
WORLD VIEW Open-mindedness/Respect for Beliefs Lifetime Learning **SOCIAL/INTERPERSONAL STYLE** Instilling Trust Adapting Socially **SITUATIONAL APPROACH** Flexibility Patience Even Disposition Navigating Ambiguity Humility Locus of Control/Initiative	--Global Networking --Driving Performance --Building Team Effectiveness

Intercultural Constructs and Competencies (Zaccaro's Proximal Attributes)

World View

Our World View category consists of two competencies of leadership behavior that demonstrates an openness to diverse ways of people and their beliefs, and a commitment to global learning.

Open-mindedness/Respecting Beliefs

Open-minded individuals are receptive to different beliefs and ideas without feeling challenged or threatened. Those with the attitude that their own or their nation's way is inherently superior face difficulties in working internationally. According to Seelye (1996), "The beginning of wisdom is the ability to see at least two sides of a story," Rhinesmith (1993) said "The first lesson in an international assignment is that your perspective is just one side of the elephant. To adjust to the new culture and be effective, you have to be willing to crawl around the elephant, understand how it looks from all sides, and be able to communicate and empathize with the people who are looking at it from the other side." This competency includes the capacity to be non-judgmental of others' spiritual and political beliefs. According to Harris and Moran (1991), "The ability to express respect for another is an important part of effective relations in every country. All people like to believe and feel that others respect them, their ideas and their accomplishments." Global leaders who demonstrate a willingness and ability to respect and be interested in beliefs of other cultures are more likely to establish meaningful intercultural relationships.

Lifetime Learning

A deep knowledge of other nations and cultures is one of the factors discovered by Tucker et al. (2004) that "differentiates those who successfully adapt to working with other cultures." This involves interest in cultural history and tradition as well as current local events. According to Walsch, Heyman, & Devaney (2008) "The ability to gain this knowledge is characteristic of those who are committed to a pattern of lifetime learning. This pattern is also important for one's career."

Social/Interpersonal Style

This category includes two competencies that enable connecting well with different kinds of people in business and social environments.

Instilling Trust

There are many benefits for the person who maintains an attitude of trust in other people. "The high-trusting person is less likely to be unhappy, conflicted, or maladjusted; he or she is liked more and is sought out as a friend more often, both by low-trusting and high-trusting others" Rotter (1980). According to Covey (2006), page 286 "The first job of a leader is to inspire trust. The ability to do so, in fact, is a prime differentiator between a manager and a leader. To inspire trust is to create the foundation upon which all truly successful enterprises – and relationships – stand." Furthermore, quoting from Black, et al. (1992),

"Trusting employees and involving them in the decision-making process results in better overall decisions, greater acceptance of decisions, and increased satisfaction in international leadership situations." Also, "The ability to develop trust among team members is an important aspect of international team performance." Tucker (2008); Cleland and Ireland (2002).

Adapting Socially

This reflects the ability to socialize with new people in unfamiliar social situations and to be accepted by new groups of people. Teagarden and Gordon (1995) explain: "Possession of technical skills may not be sufficient for successful adaptation or for information transfer, which is often considered a key strategic objective. The literature suggests that relationship skills are also important. One study found that caring about coworkers and being considerate of others predicted ability to transfer knowledge to host nationals…Still others have found that knowledge of people of other cultures, willingness to interact with them, and positive attitudes toward them are indispensable to adjustment and intercultural interaction."

Business goals are accomplished all over the world in social situations, often informally. One who feels comfortable only in small, intimate groups may feel lost in new and unfamiliar settings. This competency also includes the demonstration of interest in other people. The importance of social adaptability and interpersonal interest was stated by Kohls (1996): "Much of your effectiveness on the job and satisfaction will depend on how well you build working and social relationships with the host nationals." Those who are sincerely interested in, accepting of, and concerned for others, have a great advantage in adjusting to people of other cultures.

Situational Approach

This category includes five competencies that describe a leadership style that works well in situations where different cultural values and attitudes come into play.

Flexibility

Flexibility when working with people from other cultures is important because we all view problems and situations through thick cultural lenses. There is always more than one valid way of approaching and solving a problem; the approach and solution that we prefer is largely a matter of our cultural lens. Kohls (1996) states: "We are doomed to carry our complete load of cultural baggage wherever we go. There will be no stripping down to lighten the burden or to make the trip easier. It's important, therefore, to know as much as possible about what our culture has packed for us to carry endlessly about the world." Guy and Mattock (1996) explain "When your preparation is complete, the great thing is to be ready to adapt your methods to the local terrain. Flexible responses are part and parcel of good tactics."

The ability to consider new ideas and to acknowledge that there are multiple ways to approach and solve problems are necessary for effective global leadership. Flexibility also requires exploring new ways of doing things. The willingness to take risks, meet challenges and cope with change greatly enhances global leadership.

Patience

"Time" differs by culture. Failure to understand this may lead to frustration from unexpected delays or seemingly rash decisions. Leaders must remain patient when local business protocol demands a decision-making process or way of doing business that is unique to a certain culture. In his classic book The Silent Language, Hall (1959), explained how "time is perceived and managed differently across cultures and how patience is required to deal with these differences." Nisbitt (2003) provided a deep and thorough explanation of and description of how

Asians and Westerners think differently and why. The two fundamentally different ways of thinking require a large amount of patience in order for Asians and Westerners to relate well and work together. Aislein and Mastrin (2001) describe the French Cartesian style of thinking and decision-making, which suggests patient responses of the French to work with other cultures and vice-versa.

Even Disposition

Leading authors on the nature of leadership, Kouzes & Posner (1995); Dotlich, et al. (2009), Rhinesmith (1996); Zenger Folkman (2009), include effective interpersonal skills and understanding one's style and effect on others as core competencies. In an international environment, this means remaining calm, not being critical of oneself and exhibiting a good sense of humor. The ability to bring humor into difficult or confusing situations and to learn from one's own mistakes often helps to ease tensions and facilitate communication across cultures. As Kohls (1996) explains: "A sense of humor is important because there is going to be much to weep or get angry or annoyed or embarrassed or discouraged about. No matter how many of the other important cross-cultural skills you have, the ability to laugh things off will be the ultimate weapon against despair." Doskoch (1996) summarized associations between humor and laughter on one hand, and an amazing variety of mental and physical health benefits on the other. These included a positive mood in the face of stress, relaxation, belonging and social cohesion, creativity, and even enhanced physical immunity.

Navigating Ambiguity

Global leaders who tolerate and successfully deal with ambiguity are able to see through vagueness and uncertainty, eventually figuring out the ways of a foreign culture. They are not threatened by ambiguity or seek "black or white" solutions, but enjoy dealing with the unknown. Rhinesmith (1993) listed "the ability to feel comfortable with ambiguity" as one of the basic capacities of a global mindset. Rhinesmith continued to say, "Global management is more complex because one faces the challenge of managing increased ambiguity in decision-making. This results from being exposed to many more variables and broader issues, which often have philosophical, moral and cultural dimensions, as well as business considerations. This makes the decision process more ambiguous."

Humility

Successful global leaders engage in the processes of adjustment and overcoming challenges with a sense of humility. They realize that an egotistical, self-centered, arrogant approach is quickly rejected. People around the world appreciate leaders who ask for help, advice and information, instead of assuming that they already know as much as they need to know. Collins (2001) discussed a surprisingly consistent characteristic of leaders who took their organizations from being good to being great. Called "Level 5 Leadership," this is defined as building enduring greatness through a paradoxical blend of personal humility and professional will.

Locus of Control

"Locus of control refers to the extent to which individuals believe that they can take the initiative and control events that affect them" Rotter (1966); Ward & Kennedy (1992), Ward and Kennedy (1993). Individuals who have an internal locus of control believe that the events in their lives are generally the result of their own behavior and actions and they take responsibility for their actions. On the other hand, individuals who have an external locus of control believe that the events in their lives are generally determined by chance, fate, circumstance or other people.

Global Leader Success Criteria (Zuccaro's Leadership Criteria)

In order to meet the standard of linking intercultural competencies to performance, we settled on three performance areas, or global leader success criteria as follows:

Global networking

This criterion is defined as:

- Developing a network of international relationships.
- Making successful transitions to working with people of other nationalities.

Driving performance

This area includes:

- Evidence of effectiveness in a global leadership role.
- Team achievement of global business goals and company success in countries of operation.
- The company being seen as a preferred place to work by the local workforce.

Building team effectiveness

This area includes:

- Successful coaching of team members and developing competency.
- Building trust and a culture of respect.
- Learning from the team.

Theoretical Statement

Our Theoretical Statement is as Follows:

Intercultural competencies have a significant influence on global leadership success. There is a set of ten attributes (intercultural competencies) among global leaders that can be measured on a universal (etic) level and used on a culturally contingent (emic) level to compare competencies across cultures and to predict three separate criteria of global leadership success.

Hypotheses

The hypotheses to be tested were the following:

H1
Responses from global leaders to an intercultural competency assessment instrument will yield a set of factors with acceptable psychometric properties to confirm the ten proposed competencies.

H2
The extracted factors will assess the strengths and weaknesses of intercultural competencies among global leaders.

H3
The extracted factors will compare the strengths and weaknesses of intercultural competencies across nationalities of global leaders.

H4
Reponses from global leaders to an instrument assessing criteria of leadership success will yield a set of factors with acceptable psychometric properties to confirm three proposed success areas.

H5
The extracted criterion factors will assess the level of Success among global leaders.

H6
The extracted criterion factors will compare success across nationalities of global leaders.

H7

The extracted intercultural competency factors will predict the success criterion factors at acceptable levels of confidence.

Method

Intercultural competency assessment with the Global Leader TAP® Assessment Profile (GLTAP)

The Global Leader TAP® Assessment Profile (GLTAP) is a 107-item instrument, designed to assess the ten intercultural competencies in our model, including nine social desirability, or "fake good" items. A five-point, Likert-type scale was used to measure responses to each item (Likert 1932). The response anchors ranged from "strongly agree" to "strong disagree."

Assessment of global leadership success with the Survey of Global Business Experience (GBE)sm

This phase of the study was designed to address the criterion problem in assessment prediction research. As stated earlier, there have been a large number of leadership competencies identified and studied, but few studies have shown that these competencies lead to and predict leadership success criteria. Quoting from Guion (1998), p. 130 "The criterion problem continues to lead all other topics in lip service and to trail most in terms of work reported," and "Improved prediction cannot be expected without firm understanding of what we want to predict."

In order to address this criterion problem, leaders who had earlier completed the GLTAP completed a 12-item instrument called the "Survey of Global Business Experience (GBE)*sm*." A 20-point scale was used to measure these items, so that an item could be rated from 0 (complete lack of agreement) to 20 (compete agreement). "This scale therefore has a meaningful absolute zero point" Guilford (1965).

Participants

The GLTAP and GBE were completed on-line between April of 2010 and September of 2011. A total of 1953 leaders from a wide range of nations completed the GLTAP. Of those leaders, 1867 represented the 13 nations examined in this study. A total of 834 individuals from these 13 nations subsequently completed the GBE. Table 1 shows sample sizes for each of the 13 nations examined in this study.

Table 1 - Total Sample Size by Nationality

for GLTAP and GBE Data.

Nationality	GLTAP (N)	GLTAP and GBE (N)
Australian	189	76
Belgian	93	40
Brazilian	140	54
Canadian	192	103
Chinese	122	50
French	178	94
German	173	104
Indian	186	85
Japanese	139	41
Norwegian	67	18
Swedish	52	w
United Kingdom	175	79
American	161	58
Total N	1867	834

Jokinen's (2005) definition of global leadership competencies stated earlier guided our selection of study participants. We screened for participants who were leading across cultures, and working in many different industries. We were not concerned about different levels of responsibility. A wide variety of organizations were included, from mid-size to Fortune 100 organizations. There were 134 industries represented. Some 66% of respondents were male, 34% female (mean age = 43). Only global leaders were included in the study. Some 80 NASA International Project Managers and their international colleagues were included. We defined a global leader as one who is engaged in managing people across cultures either on international assignment or working from a home base. Responsibilities for leaders included (respondents were asked to check all that applied):

- 59% as having top executive responsibility;
- 51% as having profit and loss responsibility;
- 50% as having responsibility over a group of businesses;
- 42% as having top executive responsibility for their business function.

Analyses of GLTAP Responses

First, means were calculated on the GLTAP Social Desirability scale, and MANOVAs were conducted to determine if Social Desirability affected scores on the GLTAP competency scales (high Social Desirability scores may lead to systematically erroneous high competency scores). Next, confirmatory factor analyses (CFA) were performed on (a) the English-as-a-first language samples, and (b) the total sample in order to test the hypothesized ten factor structure. Lastly, another set of CFAs were conducted to examine the factor structure.

GLTAP Intercultural Competency Strengths and Weaknesses and Comparison Across Nationalities

Once the GLTAP factor structure was established, measurement equivalence analyses were performed to establish (a) how well the GLTAP model fit each national sample, separately, and (b) how well the GLTAP items functioned across nationalities in order for us to gain confidence the nationalities could be compared. These analyses were done by means of CFA. First we examined model fit, separately, for each of the 13 national samples. Then, we conducted a multiple groups CFA to examine configural invariance across national samples.

Analyses of GBE Responses

Confirmatory factor analyses were performed on the GBE responses to study the hypothesized three criterion success factors.

GBE Success Strengths and Weaknesses and Comparison Across Nationalities

Measurement equivalent analyses were done to determine if the GBE success factors could be compared across the nine nationalities. A factor model, along with a combined score, was used to estimate global leadership success for the total sample as well as to compare success across these nationalities. Major differences were found in the rank orders of the nationalities for the intercultural competencies as compared with the rank orders of success factors. In order to explain the results of the success factors across nationalities, a rank-order correlation was calculated for the success factor ranks and the Hofstede Power Distance Rankings (Hofstede 1997).

Predicting Leadership Success

This final step of the study method was to attempt the prediction of GBE global leadership success with the GLTAP intercultural competencies, which had been measured at an earlier point in time. Total scores on the competency factors were correlated with total scores on the success factors. An omnibus ANOVA, a test of whether all competency factor scores together predicted success scores, was performed.

A final, extreme groups analysis was conducted, whereby those who scored in the top 20% and the bottom 20% on the GBE success factors were identified. An Omnibus Test of Model Coefficients was used to predict membership in these two groups by means of the GLTAP competency factors.

Results

Social Desirability

A series of ANOVAs were conducted to examine whether individuals differed in their responses to items across the ten hypothesized factors based on social desirability scores. Cutoffs of the top 10%, 15%, and 20% were used to compare to the responses of those in the remainder of the sample. No significant differences were found using any of the cutoffs. Thus, no participant data was dropped for further analyses based on social desirability scale scores.

Analyses of GLTAP Responses
Confirmatory Factor Analysis (CFA)

Using all 98 items comprising ten hypothesized factors (social desirability items were excluded), a confirmatory factor analysis (CFA) was conducted across the English-as-a-first-language samples (i.e., Australia, Canada, United Kingdom, and United States; n = 717). This CFA did not converge, resulting in no fit statistics for the analysis. This same analysis was then conducted across the entire participant sample (N = 1,953), but again the ten factor CFA did not converge. Based on the item factor loadings and a content reanalysis we retained 51 of the original 98 items to create a more parsimonious six factor structure. We identified these factors as Respecting Beliefs (seven items; α = .82), Navigating Ambiguity (nine items; α = .80), Instilling Trust (eight items; α = .72), Adapting Socially (12 items; α = .86), Even Disposition (seven items; α = .72), and Demonstrating Creativity (eight items; α = .72).

We then used CFA to assess the six factor GLTAP structure. Across the entire sample (N = 1,953), the six factor structure did not fit the data well, $\chi2$ (1024) = 9398.87, CFI = .70, TLI = .68, RMSEA = .07, according to CFI and TLI (>.90) and RMSEA (<.08) fit standards suggested by MacDonald and Ho (2002). Based on these criteria, the six factor model did not fit the data well. In exploring the factor loadings of the six factor model it became clear items in the Adapting Socially, Even Disposition, and Demonstrating Creativity factors were not functioning as expected. In addition, one item from the Instilling Trust factor fit poorly with the other items under that factor, and was dropped from subsequent analyses. This left 23 items across three factors: Respecting Beliefs, Navigating Ambiguity, and Instilling Trust. The three-factor model, which included a higher-order "global leadership" factor, fit the data substantially better, $\chi2$ (227) = 1608.48, CFI = .89, TLI = .88, RMSEA = .06, and approached acceptable fit according to MacDonald and Ho's (2002) standards. In addition, each of the three factors loaded highly onto the higher order factor - Respecting Beliefs = 0.79, Navigating Ambiguity = 0.84, and Instilling Trust = 0.87—suggesting that each was a relatively strong indicator of the higher order construct of global leadership. We were unable to find support for Hypothesis 1 in that the proposed 10 factor model did not demonstrate acceptable model fit. However, we were able to identify a more parsimonious alternative model that demonstrated improved fit.

Measurement Equivalence for the Three Factor GLTAP Model

Next, we tested whether the three factor GLTAP model could be meaningfully compared across nationalities. We did so by conducting measurement equivalence analyses. First, we conducted a CFA of the three factor model for each national sample separately. This gave us a better understanding of how well the three factor model held up across each nationality. Second, we conducted a multiple group CFA to test for configural invariance. Here, factor loadings associated with each national sample were compared, with model fit indices indicating congruency across each nationality's factor loadings.

The results of the separate CFAs by nationality are shown in Table 2. Clearly, the data fit better among some nationalities than others. Nationalities that showed relatively better fit include: Australia, Canada, China, France, Germany, India, and the United Kingdom. Nationalities that showed relatively worse fit were Brazil, Japan, Norway, and Sweden. In the cases of the Norwegian and Swedish samples, a lack of power due to small sample sizes may have been the cause of poor fit. Surprisingly, model fit among the American sample was also lower than expected (only the RMSEA value met acceptable fit standards).

Table 2 - CFAs for Each National Sample on the GLTAP 3-Factor Model.

Nationality	N	CFI	TLI	RMSEA
Australian	189	.86	.84	.07
Belgian	93	.70	.67	.07
Brazilian	140	.41	.35	.14
Canadian	192	.83	.81	.07
Chinese	122	.81	.79	.07
French	178	.85	.84	.06
German	173	.84	.83	.07
Indian	186	.79	.77	.07
Japanese	139	.60	.55	.10
Norwegian	67	.60	.56	.11
Swedish	52	.65	.62	.13
British	175	.84	.82	.06
American	161	.69	.65	.07

After examining the results of the separate CFAs by nationality, we then conducted two multiple-group CFA models to test for configural invariance. The first model included all 13 nationalities (Model 1). Likely due to a lack of statistical power and the poor model fit found for a number of the nationalities at the previous step, Model 1 did not converge. In an attempt to remedy the latter, the nationalities with the poorest model fit, as indicated by the fit statistics shown in Table 2 (Brazilian, Japanese, Norwegian, and Swedish samples), were not included in Model 2. Model 2, which included the remaining nine national samples, showed acceptable fit, $\chi2$ (1169.56) = 227, CFI = .91, TLI = .90, RMSEA = .05. This suggests that, at least at a basic level, the items functioned in the same manner across these nine nationalities.

Given these analyses, we found support for Hypotheses 2 and 3. Specifically, we established (a) which national samples best fit the three-factor model, and (b) configural invariance, an essential estimate of measurement equivalence (Vandenberg & Lance 2000), of the three factor model across nine of the nationalities. Table 3 presents the means and standard deviations for each of the three factors, separately for each of the nine nationalities. Given that configural invariance was established across these nine nationalities, we can be more confident that scores on the three competencies can be reasonably compared across nine nationalities.

Table 3: Descriptive statistics for GLTAP – Three Factor Model.

	Instilling Trust		Respecting Beliefs		Navigating Ambiguity		Total Score	
	M	*SD*	*M*	*SD*	*M*	*SD*	*M*	*SD*
Australia	2.81	0.64	3.54	0.80	2.66	0.63	3.00	0.69
Belgium	2.86	0.45	3.18	0.60	2.85	0.57	2.96	0.54
Canada	2.85	0.64	3.43	0.73	2.69	0.62	2.99	0.66
China	2.48	0.47	2.33	0.70	2.11	0.49	2.31	0.55
France	2.60	0.48	2.76	0.61	2.52	0.64	2.63	0.58
Germany	2.76	0.53	2.99	0.70	2.70	0.60	2.82	0.61
India	2.50	0.48	2.90	0.84	2.32	0.52	2.57	0.61
United Kingdom	2.75	0.65	3.51	0.62	2.84	0.60	3.03	0.62
United States	3.49	0.48	3.71	0.62	3.07	0.59	3.42	0.56
Full Sample	2.79	0.62	3.18	0.81	2.64	0.64	2.87	0.69

The most strongly held competency by all nine nationalities (Full Sample) was Respecting Beliefs (3.18), followed by Instilling Trust (2.79) and then Navigating Ambiguity (2.64). The four figures that follow show how leaders of each of the nine nationalities compared on the competencies identified as being the strongest and consistent across nationalities.

Total of Aggregated Competencies

Overall GLTAP mean scores by nationality are shown in Figure 17. American leaders had the highest mean scores for the aggregated competencies, while the Chinese leaders had the lowest. The other seven national samples had similar mean scores.

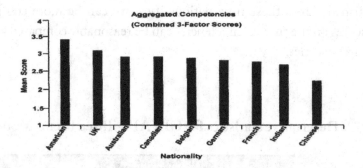

Fig. 17. Aggregated Competencies by Nationality

Respecting Beliefs

Again, the American leaders were the strongest in this competency (Figure 18), followed closely by Australian, British and Canadian leaders. The Chinese, French and Indian leaders were the least proficient in this competency.

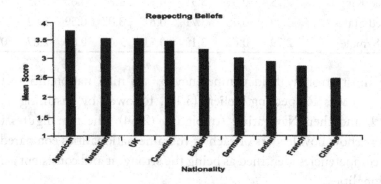

Fig. 18. Respecting Beliefs by Nationality

Navigating Ambiguity

The mean scores for this competency were not as differentiated by nationality (Figure 19).

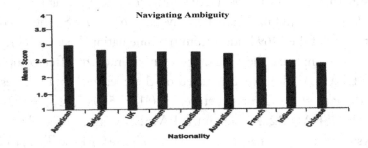

Fig. 19. Navigating Ambiguity By Nationality

However, the Americans again ranked strongest, followed by the Belgians, British and Germans.

Instilling Trust

The American leaders were far stronger in this competency than any other nationality (Figure 20). Again, the Chinese, Indians and French trailed on the lower end of the mean scores for proficiency.

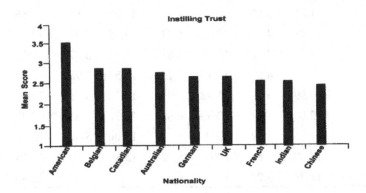

Fig. 20. Instilling Trust By Nationality

Analyses of GBE Responses

The Global Business Experience (GBE) survey measures respondents' self-reported experiences and behaviors concerning global leadership, and was used as the predictive criterion in this study. The GBE was designed to measure three factors: Global Networking (α = .78), Driving Performance (α = .91), and Building Team Effectiveness (α = .97). Six hundred and eighty-nine of the 1469 leaders from the nine nationalities with GLTAP data also completed the GBE, three to six months after completing the GLTAP. A CFA was conducted on these leaders' data to assess the hypothesized three-factor structure, $\chi2$ (51) = 560.07, CFI = .92, TLI = .90, RMSEA = .12. Although the RMSEA value associated with this analysis indicates less than acceptable fit, both the CFI and TLI produced acceptable fit standards (MacDonald & Ho, 2002), providing support for Hypothesis 4. Descriptive statistics for overall GBE scores (Success Index) and for each of the three GBE factors are presented separately for each nationality and the full sample in Table 4 (Confirmation for hypothesis 5).

Table 4: Descriptive Statistics for the GBE Across Nine Nationalities for GBE

Nationality	Global Networking		Driving Performance		Building Team Effectiveness		Success Index	
	M	SD	M	SD	M	SD	M	SD
Australia	10.00	6.44	10.02	6.66	10.34	7.05	10.12	6.72
Belgium	11.76	5.11	12.72	4.21	14.11	3.64	12.86	4.32
Canada	11.83	4.6	12.38	4.42	13.08	4.48	12.43	4.50
China	14.39	3.48	14.55	3.08	14.52	3.27	14.49	3.28
France	12.21	4.82	12.74	4.18	13.57	3.93	12.84	4.31
Germany	10.59	5.55	11.42	5.09	12.32	4.93	11.44	5.19
India	12.81	5.24	13.53	4.62	13.77	4.53	13.37	4.80
UK	12.56	5.54	12.23	5.22	13.06	5.43	12.62	5.40
US	13.09	5.8	12.66	5.82	13.8	5.73	13.18	5.78
Total Sample	11.98	5.21	12.35	4.86	13.04	4.84	12.46	4.97

Measurement Equivalence Analysis for the GBE

As with the GLTAP data, separate CFAs were conducted for each nationality on the three factor GBE model. The fit statistics for each nationality are in Table 5. Following the CFAs conducted separately for each national sample, a multiple groups CFA was conducted to test for configural invariance across all nine nationalities, $\chi2$ (459) = 1317.86, CFI = .88, TLI = .85, RMSEA = .16. This shows CFI and TLI indices approach acceptable fit standards, while the RMSEA value associated with this model falls well outside of acceptable standards. Taken together, there appears to be configural noninvariance between nationalities (Hypothesis 6).

Table 5: GBE CFAs by Nationality.

Nationality	CFI	TLI	RMSEA
Australian	0.90	0.87	0.17
Belgian	0.92	0.90	0.12
Canadian	0.92	0.89	0.12
Chinese	0.86	0.81	0.16
French	0.94	0.92	0.11
German	0.85	0.81	0.17
Indian	0.88	0.85	0.18
UK	0.83	0.78	0.19
American	0.84	0.79	0.15

Success Factors Compared Across Nationalities

Figures 21, 22, 23 and 24 show how leaders of each of the nine nationalities compared on the success factors. Note that GBE responses were made using a 0 to 20 scale, but that these figures reflect a smaller portion of the scale in order to illustrate differences.

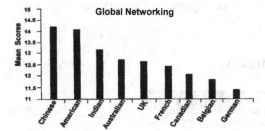

Fig. 21 Global Networking by Nationality

Fig. 22 Driving Performance by Nationality

Fig. 23 Building Team Effectiveness

Fig. 24 Global Leader Success Index by Nationality

73

Interestingly, the rank order of GBE scores by nationality is quite different than those for the GLTAP intercultural competencies. For example, Chinese respondents ranked lowest on each of the GLTAP competencies, and highest on the success index and on 2 of the 3 success factors. Indian and French respondents also ranked higher on GBE success factors than on GLTAP factors. We discuss possible explanations of these differences in rank order in the Discussion section.

Predictive Validity of the GLTAP
Multilevel Modeling

The initial approach to determine how well the GLTAP competency factors predict the GBE success criteria was to use multilevel modeling (MLM), wherein individual respondents are nested within nationality. This approach allows both the variance due to individual differences (i.e., within-nationality) and group-based differences (i.e., between-nationality) in the data to be modeled. However, we found that over 96% of the variance in the data was due to within-nationality differences, meaning that only less than 4% of variance in the data was due to differences between nationalities. Because the amount of variance associated with between-nationality differences was minimal, there was little value in the use of MLM over the more widely used and less statistically complex multiple linear regression (MLR) approach. Thus, we proceeded using MLR.

Multiple Linear Regression

We were unable to support the construct validity of the six-factor GLTAP through CFA. However, the primary use of these six factors is for predicting relevant criteria. Thus, we determined it important to assess the criterion-related validity of all six factors. First, we examined overall GLTAP scores predicting overall GBE scores. $R = .22$ $R2 = 4.80\%$, $F1 = 34.94$, $p < .001$, $\beta = 24.23$, $p < .001$. Next, we included each of the six factor scores as separate predictors, in order to assess the criterion-related validity of separate factor scores when included in a single model. The results of the overall model are as follows: $R = .29$ $R2 = 8.30\%$, $F6 = 10.26$, $p < .001$. These results show that the six factor GLTAP model significantly predicted GBE success scores.

Extreme Groups Analysis

Next we assessed the predictive validity of the GLTAP competency factors in predicting the GBE criteria using an extreme groups analysis approach. Twenty percent of those who scored highest (N=141) and lowest on the GBE (N=143) were identified for comparison. Using hierarchical logistic regression, we predicted group membership (high GBE scores/ low GBE scores) with respondents' scores on the three GLTAP factors established through CFA: Respecting Beliefs, Navigating Ambiguity, and Instilling Trust. Based on GLTAP factor scores, 55% of those with the highest GBE scores and 54% of those with the lowest GBE scores were correctly identified in the model. We then added the three additional factors from the initially proposed six-factor model: Adapting Socially, Even Disposition, and Demonstrating Creativity. The six-factor model correctly classified 67% of those with the top 20% of GBE scores and 73% of those with the lowest 20% GBE scores, a substantial improvement on the three factor model, $\chi2$ (6, N = 284) = 49.29, p < .001. Therefore, applying the six factor model represents a 46% improvement in predicting success and a 34% improvement in predicting failure among global leaders. This result is illustrated in figure 25.

Figure 25. Competencies Predicting Leadership Success

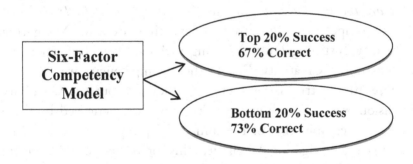

These results demonstrate that scores on the six GLTAP factors can be fairly effective at differentiating those with the highest and lowest GBE success scores, and the use of scores on all six proposed factors is more effective at correctly predicting group membership than scores on the three factors established based on CFA. Taken together, findings from predictive analyses provide support for Hypothesis 7.

Discussion

In the present study we sought to assess the validity of the GLTAP as an measure of global leadership competencies. We failed to find support for the initially proposed model, yet we identified a more parsimonious model demonstrating improved factorial validity. We then identified a subset of nationalities across which evidence indicates the equivalent functioning of the GLTAP factor structure. Next, we validated the factor structure of the GBE across the sample, but failed to demonstrate the equivalent functioning of the criterion measure across nationalities. Nonetheless, we found overall GLTAP and factor scores accounted for a modest amount of variance in GBE success scores, and six GLTAP factor scores showed to be effective in identifying respondents whose GBE success scores were among those in the top and bottom 20% of distribution in our sample. We describe each finding in greater depth below.

This study set out to provide answers to six questions regarding intercultural competencies of global leaders. Discussion of the study is organized here according to these questions.

What are the intercultural competencies among global leaders? A set of six competencies emerged: Respecting Beliefs; Navigating Ambiguity; Instilling Trust; Adapting Socially; Even Disposition and Demonstrating Creativity. Five of these competencies were similar to those 10 constructs that were hypothesized, but the Creativity dimension was a new discovery. Creativity was perceived by these leaders as a combination of Flexibility, Adapting Socially, Lifetime Learning and Navigating Ambiguity. This competency could therefore be viewed as "Social and Situational Creativity."

The psychometric strengths of these six competencies, and the large sample size comprised exclusively of global leaders, provides confidence that these can be used for global leadership assessment and development, and for further research.

These Six Factors are Described Below in Terms of Leadership Competencies *Respecting Beliefs (RB – 7 items)*

This competency represents a leader's ability to demonstrate respect for the political and spiritual beliefs of people in other cultures. It also includes a good sense of humor, which is an often mentioned but underappreciated, aspect of global leadership. Leaders who can use appropriate humor in tense situations involving political or spiritual differences can diffuse tensions and loosen things up for more successful problem solving. This competency focuses on respecting beliefs, which can be very sensitive across cultures, particularly when it comes to politics and spiritual beliefs. Those in global leadership roles must be careful in both verbal and non-verbal messages to not only avoid disrespectful comments, but to learn enough about the beliefs of their people to show respect (such as acknowledging important dates and ceremonies).

While it is essential that global business leaders understand and remain abreast of the political environments in the countries where they operate, they must be sensitive to deeply held political beliefs. The wide gulf in the current American political scene, and the difficulties faced by members of the European Union, present subjects that are rife for passionate debate but would be wise to be avoided by global business leaders.

With respect to spiritual beliefs for example, in Africa a leader must recognize the importance of extended family death rituals and accommodate employee leave times for funerals.

Another example is, in Muslim societies, a leader must adjust organizational life to the five pillars of Islam, including the five daily prayers.

Navigating Ambiguity (NA 9 items)

This competency represents a leader's ability to see through vagueness and uncertainty, not become frustrated, and figure out how things are done in other cultures. Ambiguous situations are the norm in leading across cultures, so that the ability to work successfully in these environments is truly an advantage.

One way that leaders express this competency is by avoiding the concept of "Misattribution of Motives and Behavior." When confronted with foreign ways, people naturally tend to attribute what is seen and heard based one's own cultural background. Leaders from cultures with a low-context or direct style of communication, for instance, may find the long and circular process of decision-making characteristic of more indirect, high context cultures frustrating and ambiguous. These leaders (mainly from Western cultures) may attribute this to disagreement with their own plan or proposal among their (Asian) counterparts, or to poor decision-making capability. The correct attribution is that longer decision-making for their counterparts is culturally natural for them and involves more stakeholders and leads to quicker implementation.

Instilling Trust (IT 8 items)

This competency represents a leader's ability to build and maintain trusting relationships. Extensive research and practice among global teams concludes that trust is the one glue that holds these diverse teams together. Building and maintaining trust across cultures is a complicated process, because trust does not mean the same thing to members of different cultures. Successful global leaders take the time to understand these cultural differences among their people and to build and maintain trust in appropriate ways. According to Covey and Merrill (2006), "Low levels of trust typically slow down everything—every decision, every communication, and every relationship. On the other hand, high trust produces speed. Leaders who bring high trust to multicultural organizations get superior results by clarifying expectations, listening first, creating transparency and practicing accountability."

Adapting Socially (AS 12 items)

This competency represents a leader's ability to socialize comfortably with new people in unfamiliar social situations and to demonstrate genuine interest in other people. Many studies have shown that Adapting Socially is a powerful predictor of intercultural adjustment. Much of global business takes place in social situations, over food and drink, and leaders who can recognize and engage appropriately in these situations are more successful than those who don't. An important aspect of this competency is showing interest in other people. Remembering and correctly pronouncing names, as well as remembering and repeating things learned about others are ways to do this.

A critical lesson that global businesses have learned in order to succeed in Asia is that networking and relationship building is the essence of Asian business cultures. Leaders who have a high Adapting Socially competence recognize this and are able to do this. This approach is quite different, for example, for Western retailers who want to succeed with sourcing in Asia. They are not used to building relationships with their domestic suppliers, relying instead on requiring the best products at the lowest price. They can do this as well in Asia, but with much more long-term success and loyalty through networking and relationship building with their Asian suppliers.

Even Disposition (ED 7 items)

This competency represents a leaders ability to remain calm, not being critical of oneself and learning from mistakes. In good times and especially in bad, people in an organization look to their leaders for guidance. Those leaders who take things in stride and maintain an even disposition set a tone for the organization culture that is resilient.

Demonstrating Creativity (DC 8 items)

This competency represents a leaders ability to enjoy new challenges, strive for innovative solutions to social and situational issues and to learn from a variety of sources. This quality includes the ability to see around corners, predict outcomes and act despite uncertainty. This dimension of creativity is therefore related to the Navigating Ambiguity dimension discussed above. Creative approaches are more difficult, but more successful, in ambiguous situations.

Creative global leaders practice and encourage experimentation and innovation throughout their organizations. They expect to make deeper business model changes to realize their strategies, take more calculated risks, find and support new ideas, and keep innovating in how they lead and communicate. Successful global leadership is all about leading through others, finding creative ways to select, retain and motivate diverse talent. It is also about maintaining a competitive, creative edge through lifetime learning—making a habit of learning from a variety of sources.

What are the strongest of these competencies and those in need of greatest development?

Equivalence analyses showed that three of the competencies could be compared across cultures. Of these, Respecting Beliefs was the strongest. This is encouraging, given the volatile situation involving spiritual and political differences in the world today. Leaders who can maintain a focus on organizational issues, while demonstrating an understanding and respect for the diversity of beliefs in his or her global organization, are certainly in great need. An interesting aspect of this competency was a value on the use of humor to diffuse tense or stressful situations. This is an often overlooked aspect of successful leadership, but one that is quickly recognized and appreciated in those leaders who use humor appropriately.

Instilling Trust and Navigating Ambiguity were rated lowest of the three competencies. This is not surprising, given the complexity of trust and its meaning across cultures, and the fact that global business operates in much more of a grey area than black-and white.

A total score of all three competencies had a mean of only 2.86 on a five-point scale, indicating that these leaders have some way to go for full development of these competencies. These results support the surveys and studies cited in the Introduction to this book, that global organizations do not have the leaders needed to keep up with the speed of business, are not satisfied with the quality of their leaders, and do not have the bench strength to meet future business needs. This study points to specific areas to meet these needs.

How do these competencies differ across nationalities?

The American leaders had the highest mean scores for the aggregated list of competencies, followed by the British and Australian leaders, while the Chinese leaders had the lowest with the French and Indian leaders trailing close behind.

Explanations for these differences can only come from an in-depth look at each nationality, its business culture, and how these differ from one another. One issue may be that Chinese, French and Indian leaders have different understandings of the meaning associated with these competency factors than leaders of other nationalities. However, several useful and logical explanations follow. It may be that the American, British and Australian (the three nationalities with the highest GLTAP overall mean scores) business cultures have been greatly affected in recent years by initiatives in the areas of inclusion and cultural awareness. Canadians (fourth highest GLTAP overall mean score) celebrate multiculturalism and it is a source of national pride. Also, leaders in these four cultures have a fairly long history of working in multinational businesses, while those in China and India are quite new to this. Chinese leaders are more experienced with leading Chinese state-owned enterprises than they are with multinational companies. Indian leaders are more experienced with leading large family-owned businesses and Indian state-owned businesses than they are with multinational companies.

The Chinese, Indians and French trailed on the lower end of the mean scores for the Navigating Ambiguity proficiency. The Chinese culture is high on "uncertainty avoidance," (Hofstede, 1997) which is not surprising given the country's history of authoritarian rule. Therefore, any areas of ambiguity need to be clearly laid out for them with specific steps and actions in how to get through it. This may partially explain why the Chinese scored the lowest on the Navigating Ambiguity competency.

Differences in the competency of Instilling Trust by nationality may be partially explained by the concept of "tight" and "loose" cultures. Gunia, et al. (2011); Yamagishi and colleagues (Takahashi et al. 2008; Yamagishi et al. 1998; Yamagishi & Yamagishi 1994). Tight cultures are those in which social norms are clearly defined and reliably imposed, leaving little room for improvisation or interpretation. Loose cultures are those in which social norms are flexible and informal. They propose expectations but permit individuals to define the range of tolerable behavior within which they may exercise their own preferences. Thus, enforcement in loose cultures is left to interpersonal mechanisms. According to Gunia, et al. (2011) this concept may be applied to trust as follows: "Because institutional mechanisms govern behavior in tight cultures, individuals from these cultures tend to rely on institutional trust more than interpersonal trust to control behavior and sanction deviance. Because interpersonal mechanisms govern behavior in loose cultures, the exact opposite is true." Yamagishi (2009) asserted that people in cultures with strong social norms "do not need social intelligence to find out who is trustworthy—trust is not needed."

Applying this concept to the differences among national leaders with respect to the Instilling Trust competency, it is expected that the Chinese and Indians, and to some extent, the French, who all scored low on Instilling Trust, would represent tight cultures, while the Americans, Belgians, Canadians and Australians, who scored high on Instilling Trust, would represent loose cultures Gelfand, et al. (2011) presented tightness scores for thirty-three nationalities, including the following (the higher the score, the more "tight" the culture):

- Indian = 11
- Chinese = 7.9
- French = 6.3
- American = 5.1
- Belgian = 5.6
- Australian = 4.4

These tightness/looseness scores may therefore mean that the Indian leaders especially, and also the Chinese and French, have lower competencies on Instilling Trust because they represent tight cultures as compared with the loose cultures of the Americans, Belgians and Australians. The Indian, Chinese and French leaders rely more on assumed norms regarding trust, while the American, Belgian and Australian leaders take individual action, responsibility and accountability to instill trust among their people. These findings have an important message for the Indian, Chinese and French leaders who are leading multicultural organizations. They need to learn what trust means among the cultures of their people, and spend time and energy to develop trust as a central, expressed value in their organizations.

What are the areas of greatest leadership success?

Factor structure supported a three factor model (Hypotheses 3). However, we failed to establish configural invariance (Hypothesis 4), suggesting that these factors may reflect different constructs across nationalities. This evidence impairs the factorial validity of the GBE, yet there are multiple types of validity (see Messick 1989), and in the case of the GLTAP and GBE it could be argued that whether they work (criterion-related validity) may be more important than how they work (factorial validity). Thus, we subsequently used the GBE to test the criterion-related validity of GLTAP factor scores.

The highest rated success score was for Building Team Effectiveness. One thing that is very clear about the global business environment is that everyone works in one or more teams, either on a virtual basis or face-to-face. A large body of work has emerged to support this teamwork (Larson & LaFasto 1989; LaFasto & Larson 2001; Ray & Bronstein 1995; Parker 1994). Apparently, the leaders in this study have benefitted from this attention to team effectiveness and rate themselves relatively high on their ability to lead global teams.

Similar to the finding for intercultural competencies, a total score on all three factors of leadership success had a mean of only 13.33 on a

20-point scale, indicating that these leaders see significant room for improvement. Also, the psychometric strengths of these three factors, and the large sample size comprised exclusively of global leaders, provides confidence that these can be used as criterion measures for global leadership assessment and development and for further research.

How do these success factors differ across nationalities?

Equivalence analyses showed some evidence that this three-factor model could be compared across nationalities. Comparisons should be considered as general relative rankings, therefore, before we cannot be sure that leaders from these countries interpreted GBE items in the same manner as respondents from other countries. Overall, the Chinese had the highest mean scores, followed by the Americans, Indians, Australians and French. The rank order pattern of these success factors is quite different from that for the intercultural competencies. The Chinese had ranked lowest of the nine nationalities on the competencies, and highest on the success factors. The Indians and French also ranked higher on these success factors. One reason behind this might be that those nationalities that ranked lower on the global competencies and higher on the self-rated success factors may not have a realistic handle on the outside world's perception of them and the reality of their own performance. Also, the German leaders may have scored lowest on these success factors because of their tendency not to overstate their accomplishments, and to focus very specifically on the metrics of the GBE instrument.

A possible interpretation of this phenomenon might be found in Hofstede's Power Distance concept (Hofstede 1997). Power Distance is defined as: *The degree to which inequality or distance between those in charge and the less powerful (subordinates) is accepted in a culture.*

A high Power Distance culture favors a leadership style that is hierarchical, while a low Power Distance culture favors a participative style. Table 6 compares the success rankings with the relative rankings of these nine nationalities on Power Distance. (These are not Hofstede's original rankings. They are the relative rankings of these nine nationalities, based on the Hofstede data).

Power Distance Rankings (Large to Small)	Leadership Success Rankings (High to Low)
1. China	1. Chinese
2. India	2. American
3. France	3. Indians
4. Belgium	4. Australian
5. USA	5. French
6. Australia	6. Belgian
7. Canada	7. British
8.5. Great Britain	8. Canadian
8.5. Germany	9. German

Table 6. Power Distance and Leadership Success.

A highly significant rank order correlation was found between these two sets of rankings (r = .804), indicating that the larger Power Distance nationalities were also ranking higher on leadership success factors, and vise-versa (with the notable exception of the Americans). It may be that a characteristic of large Power Distance (hierarchical) leaders is to consider themselves and their organizations as more successful than small Power Distance (participative) leaders. They have achieved the highest levels of their organizations and may be less aware of their subordinates and others' view of their leadership success.

A final comment here is that our two instruments were completed in English and the items were not subjected to cross-language/culture adjustments for construct, method and item bias. However, we think that the clear differences on the competency and success factors were probably due to Power Distance and tight/loose cultures and not that some nationalities are less familiar with psychometric instruments. One would conclude that if they are less familiar with psychometric instruments, their results would be random, and not display the statistical differences we found.

Which competencies are most strongly predictive of leadership success?

The six factor GLTAP model significantly predicted GBE success scores. Further, when those in the top and bottom 20% of the distribution of GBE scores were selected for extreme group analyses, both the three-factor and six-factor GLTAP models were significant predictors of group membership (top 20%/bottom 20% of GBE scores), and despite our failure to find evidence supporting the factorial validity for the six-factor model, it demonstrated a substantial improvement over the three-factor model in terms of predicting group membership. Thus, the six-factor model may have greater practical utility than three-factor model. The predictive model is shown in Figure 26, which is also our modified Transcultural Leadership Model.

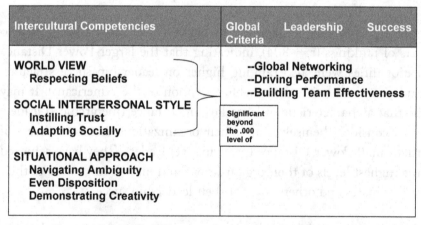

Fig. 26 Modified Transcultural Leadership Model

Contribution to Leadership Theory

As described earlier, a goal of this study was to apply Zaccaro's (2007) trait-based model of leader effectiveness to the context of global leadership and specify a set of global leadership-relevant proximal attributes. This study identified six potential intercultural competencies as proximal attributes of effective global leaders. These intercultural competencies are influenced by leader traits, and both leader traits and competencies are theorized to affect leader processes. In addition, the global business environment within which the leader is operating is believed to directly influence intercultural competencies and leaders' processes, as well as the competency-process and process criteria relationships. The way we have therefore modified the Zaccaro model appears in Figure 27.

Fig. 27 Modified Global Leader Performance Model.

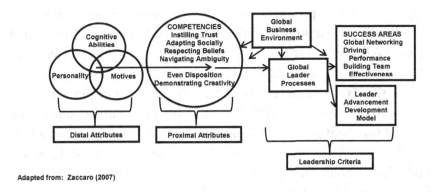

Adapted from: Zaccaro (2007)

As shown in Figure 27 above, we are therefore stating the following theoretical proposition regarding successful global leadership:

- Distal Attributes: successful global leaders most certainly have a high level of cognitive abilities; perhaps some personality traits such as extroversion, curiosity and relationship management; and a set of motives and values that drive a personal interest in other cultures.

- Proximal Attributes: we have identified six measurable intercultural competencies which interact with distal attributes

87

in important ways that lead to successful global leader performance. For example, a leader with a high level of cognitive ability without the competency of dealing with intercultural ambiguity would not be very successful in the global business environment.

- Leader Effectiveness: we have identified three measurable global leader success factors that comprise leader effectiveness in the global business environment.

Limitations, Further Research, and Practical Implications

As with all research, there are a number of limitations associated with this study. First, both the GLTAP and the GBE were completed in English. Although all respondents were senior leaders in positions requiring interaction with foreign cultures and all leaders indicated English as either a primary or secondary language, leaders' proficiency with English was unknown. This may have led to the misinterpretation of GLTAP and/or GBE items, or the inability to interpret items at all. Consequently, this may have led to increased measurement error within the data and negatively affected our attempts to establish the factorial validity of the GLTAP and GBE. For example, our failure to establish configural invariance in the GBE across nationalities may have resulted from measurement error due to a English language difficulties among some participants. Further attempts to validate the GLTAP and GBE may find it useful to: assess respondents' English proficiency with a single question (e.g., "Please rate your English using the following scale"), ensure respondents used in future analyses possess adequate proficiency with the English language, or provide versions of the measure in respondents native language.

Second, this study lacked the statistical power necessary to fully assess the factorial validity of the GLTAP. With regard to the GLTAP, larger samples will be necessary in order to conduct meaningful measurement invariance analyses in the future, and as the use of the GLTAP becomes more widespread sufficient samples to conduct these and other validity analyses will become possible.

These findings provide important practical implications. This study has resulted in a set of intercultural competencies that may be used for global talent assessment and development.

Summary of Study One

This study provides an initial attempt to validate the GLTAP and GBE. Sufficient factor structures were established for both measures. GLTAP factor scores accounted for a modest amount of variance in GBE scores across the entire sample, and the six factor scores of the GLTAP, together, appear to be effective at differentiating those who self-reported being the most successful global leaders from those who reported the lowest global leadership success scores. This study also describes the role of the GLTAP and GBE within a broader global leadership development program. Successful global leaders therefore emerge from this research as those who:

- Enjoy new challenges, strive for innovative solutions to social and situational issues and learn from a variety of sources;

- Build and maintain trusting relationships;

- Socialize comfortably with new people in unfamiliar social situations, demonstrate genuine interest in other people; and exhibit a good sense of humor;

- See through vagueness and uncertainty, do not become frustrated, and figure out how things are done in other cultures;

- Remain calm, without being critical of oneself;

- Demonstrate respect for the political and spiritual beliefs of people of other cultures.

STUDY TWO: Additional Research – A Nine Competency Model

In addition to the study described above, we had the opportunity to administer our Global Leader TAP® Assessment Profile (GLTAP) to two additional groups of leaders. One was a total of 199 NASA International Project Managers and their international partners. The lead author was the senior faculty member for the International Project Management Program (IPM) delivered at the Kennedy Space Center in Florida. The GLTAP was part of an assessment and development module delivered by the lead author.

The second group was comprised of 238 leaders of a global corporation. The GLTAP was administered to them as part of an assessment and development program.

The total sample for these two groups was therefore 437 representing 32 different nationalities. We combined these GLTAP responses with those of the 1469 representing 9 nationalities from the first study. Some 26 of this combined sample were eliminated from further analysis because of high scores on the Social Desirability Scale, which detects "fake good" responses where an attempt is made to guess the correct response instead of true judgements. We therefore had a combined sample of 1880 leaders of 41 nationalities.

The responses were examined to see if a set of competencies larger and more meaningful and useful than the original six could be defined. A set of nine competencies were produced and the data set was subjected to an item/competency correlation and estimates of alpha reliability. The GLTAP instrument measuring these competencies contains 86 items, including a Social Desirability Scale. The resulting nine competency model was presented earlier in figure 2.

CHAPTER 6

Conclusion

With this book we have aspired to address the need for more effective assessment and development of global leaders where key competencies are identified, the motivation for change is established and a clear, customized, action plan for change is created.

We have presented empirical studies of global leaders, producing a set of nine intercultural competencies that predict global leadership success. These competencies were incorporated into the H (Horizontal) part of a new HV Model of Global Leadership Development. It was shown that horizontal competency development is powerful and remains important, but is not enough. Our HV Model adds a Vertical approach focused on mental complexity in which Behavior Change Maps are presented for all nine competencies (based on the work of Kegan and Lahey in their book Immunity to Change). We also discussed application strategies for this model and some of the challenges related to the change and transition process including resistance to change. This model can lead to powerful behavior change and development of the key competencies required to lead successfully across cultures

The HV approach to global leadership development is not an "easy fix" that can be accomplished by checking some boxes. It requires an acceptance of the need for change by the leaders involved and a commitment to a sometimes difficult and uncomfortable foray into new territory.

REFERENCES

American Psychologist (2007). Vol 62 No 1. Special Issue: Leadership. Pg. 51

Asselin, Gilles & Mastron, Ruth (2001) *Au contraire! Figuring out the French.* Yarmouth, Main: The Intercultural Press. Pgs. 23, 58

Bennett, M. (1993). Towards Ethnorelitivism: A developmental model of intercultural sensitivity. In R. Paige (Ed.) *Education for the Intercultural Experience* (2nd ed., pp 21 – 71) Yarmouth, ME. Intercultural Press. Pg. 24

Bird, Allan, In Mendenhall, M. E., Osland, J. S., Bird, A. Oddou, G.R. & Maznevski, M. L. (2008). *Global leadership: Research, practice and development.* London and New York: Routledge. Pg. 52

Black, J.S., Gregerson, H.B., & Mendenhall, M.E. (1992). *Global assignments.* San Francisco, CA: Jossey Bass. Pg. 56

Boatman, J. & Wellins, R.S. (2011). *Time for a leadership revolution.* Bridgeville, PA.: DDI. Pg. 48

Bridges, William (1991). *Managing Transitions; Making the Most of Change.* Addison-Wesley. Pg. 43

Cleland, David I. and Ireland, Lewis R. (2002) Project management: *Strategic design and implementation* (4th Ed.) New York, NY: McGraw-Hill. Pg. 56

Collins, J. (2001). *Good to great.* New York: Harper Collins. Pgs. 48, 59

Covey, Stephen M.R. with Merrill, Rebecca R. *The speed of trust: The one thing that changes everything.* (2006). 1230 Avenue of the Americans New York, NY: Free Press, Simon and Schuster. Pgs. 39, 56, 81

Dickson, M.W., Den Hartog, D.N., Michelson, J.K. (2003). Research on leadership in a cross-cultural context: Making progress, and raising new questions. *The Leadership Quarterly 14 729-768*. Pg. 49

Dorfman, P.W. (2003). International and cross-cultural leadership research. B.J. Punnett, & O. Shenkar (Eds.), *Handbook for international management research* (2nd ed.). Ann Arbor, MI: University of Michigan. Pg. 49

Doskoch, Peter (1996) *Humor me: Is laughter really the best medicine?* The Los Angeles Syndicate. Pg. 58

Dotlich, David L., Cairo, Peter C. & Rhinesmith, Stephen H. (2009) *Leading in times crisis.* San Francisco, CA: Jossey-Bass. Pg. 58

Dweck, Carol S. (2006). *Mindset – The new psychology of success.* Ballantine Books, a Division of Random House, Inc., New York, New York. Pgs. 14, 16, 42, 43

Gelfand, M.J., (2011) *Science* 332 27 May. Pg. 86

Gelfand, M.J., Raver, J., Nishii, L., Leslie, Kl, Lun, J., Lim, B.C., Yan, X. (2010). The difference between "tight" and "loose" societies revisited: Ecological, social-political, and societal correlates of tightness-looseness in modern nations. *Manuscript submitted for publication.* Pg. 86

Guilford, J.P. (1965) *Fundamental statistics in psychology and education.* New York, NY: McGraw-Hill. Pg. 63

Guion, R.M. (1998). *Assessment, measurement, and prediction for personnel decisions.* Mahwah, NJ: Lawrence Erlbaum Associates. Pg. 63

Gunia, Brian C., Brett, Jeanne M., Nandkeolyar, Avit K., & Kamdur, Dishan (2011). Paying a Price: Culture, Trust, and Negotiation Consequences. *Journal of Applied Psychology,* 96, No 4, 774-789. Pg. 85

Guy, V., & Mattock, J. (1996). *The international business book*. Lincolnwood, IL: NTC Publishing Group. Pg. 57

Hall, Edward T. (1959) *The silent language*. New York, NY: Doubleday. Pg. 57

Harris, P.R., & Moran, R.T. (1991). *Managing cultural differences* (3rd Ed.). Houston, TX: Gulf Publishing Company. Pg. 55

Hawes, F., & Kealey, D.J. (1981). An empirical study of Canadian

technical assistance: Adaptation and effectiveness on overseas assignment. International *Journal of Intercultural Relations, 5*, 239-258. Pg. 53

House, R., Javidan, M., Hanges, P., & Dorfman, P. (2002).

Understanding cultures and implicit leadership theories across the globe: An introduction to project GLOBE. *Journal of World Business, 37*, 3-10. Pg. 49

Hofstede, G. (1997). *Cultures and organizations: Software of the mind*. New York: McGraw-Hill. Pgs. 66, 85, 88

House, R.J., Wright, N.S., &Aditya, R.N. (1997). Cross-cultural research on organizational leadership: A critical analysis and a proposed theory. In P.D. Earley, & M. Erez (Eds.), *New perspectives on international industrial/organizational psychology* (pp. 535-625). San Francisco, CA: Jossey-Bass. Pg. 49

IBM (2011) *Capitalizing on complexity: Insights from the Global Chief Executive Officer Study*. IBM Institute for Business Values. Pg. 48

Jokinen, T. (2005) "Global leadership competencies: a review and discussion." *Journal of European Industrial Training, 29* (2/3): 199 – 216. Pgs. 53, 64

Kegan, R. (1982). *The evolving self: Problem and process in human development.* Cambridge, MA: Harvard University Press. Pg. 17

Kegan, R. (1994). *In over our heads: The mental demands of modern life.* Cambridge, MA: Harvard University Press.

http://developmentalobserver.blog.com/2010/06/09/an-overview-of-constructive-developmental-theory-cdt/. Pgs. 17, 19

Kegan, R. & Lahey L. (2009). Immunity to Change. How to overcome it and unlock potential in yourself and your organization. Boston: *Harvard Business School Press.* Pgs. 4, 5, 17, 18, 19, 20, 36, 95

Kohls, L.R. (1996). *Survival kit for overseas living* (3rd Ed.), Yarmouth, ME: Intercultural Press. Pgs. 56, 57, 58

Kouzes, James M. Posner, Barry Z (1995) *The leadership challenge.* San Francisco, CA: Jossey-Bass. Pg. 58

Kühlmann, T., & Stahl, G. (1998). Diagnose interkultureller Kompetenz: Entwicklung und Evaluierung eines Assessment Centers. In C. Barmeyer, & J. Bolten (Eds.) Interkulturelle Personalorganisation. Berlin: Verlag Wissenschaft Praxis: 213-223. Pg. 49

LaFasto, Frank M.J., & Larson, Carl E. (2001). *When teams work best.* Thousand Oaks, CA: SAGE. Pg. 87

Larson, C.E., LaFasto, F.M.J. (1989). *Teamwork: What must go right/what can go wrong.* Sage Publications, Inc. Pg. 87

Lewin, Kurt (June, 1947). "Frontiers in Group Dynamics: Concept, Method and Reality in Social Science, Social Equilibria and Social Change." Human Relations.

Likert (1932). A technique for the measurement of attitudes. *New York Archives of Psychology,* 22 (140). Pg. 62

Lublin, J.S. (2011) Hunt is on for fresh executive talent. *The Wall Street Journal*, Monday, April 11, 2011. p. B1. Pg. 48

Macdonald, R.P., & Ho, M.R. (2002). Principles and practice in reporting structural equation analyses. *Psychological Methods, 7*, 64-82. Pgs. 66, 67, 68

McCall, M., & Hollenbeck, G. (2002). *Developing global executives: The lessons of international experience.* Boston, MA: Harvard Business School Publishing. Pg. 50

McKinsey (2012). *Managing at global scale: McKinsey Global Survey Results.* London, England: McKinsey. Pg. 4

Mendenhall, ME, Osland, JS, Bird, A. Oddou, Mazneuski, Mi (2008). *Global Leadership Research Practice and Development*, Routledge. Pgs. 4, 48, 49

Messick, S. (1989). Validity. In R. L. Linn (Ed.), *Educational measurement* (3rd ed., pp. 13-103). New York: Macmillan. Pg. 86

Nisbitt, Richard E. (2003) *The geography of thought.* New York, NY: Free Press. Pg. 58

Osland, J.S. and Bird, A. (2006) Global leaders as experts. In W. Mobely and E. Weldon (eds). *Advances in Global Leadership*, vol. 4, Stamford, CT: JAI Press: 123-152. Pg. 48

Parker, G. (1994). *Cross-functional teams.* San Francisco: Jossey-Bass. Pg. 87

Peterson, M.F., & Hunt, J.G. (1997). International perspectives on international leadership. *The Leadership Quarterly*, 8 (3), 203 -231. Pg. 49

Petrie, N. (2011). Future Trends in Leadership Development. A White Paper. *Center for Creative Leadership.* Greensboro, North Carolina. Pgs. 4, 8, 21

Pruyn, P.W. "An Overview of Constructive Developmental Theory." Developmental Observer, June 9, 2010. http://developmentalobserver. blog.com/2010/06/09/an-overview-of-constructive-developmental-theory-cdt/ accessed Dec,10, 2015. Pg. 17

Ray & Bronstein, R. (1995). *Teaming up.* McGraw Hill. Pg. 87

Rhinesmith, S.H. (1993). *A manager's guide to globalization: Six keys to success in a changing world.* Alexandria, VA: Richard Irwin, Inc. Pgs. 55, 58

Rhinesmith, Stephen H. (1996). *A Manager's Guide to Globalization.* 2nd Edition McGraw-Hill. Pg. 19

Right Management (2011) Why Global Leaders Succeed and Fail. *Insights from CEOs and Human Resources Professionals.* 1818 Market Street, Philadelphia, PA. Pg. 48

Rotter, J.B. (1966) Generalized expectancies for internal versus external control of reinforcement. *Psychological Monographs,* 80, 1 – 28. Pg. 59

Rotter, J.B. (1980) Interpersonal trust, trustworthiness, and gullibility. *American Psychologist,* 35, 1 – 7. Pg. 56

Seelye, H.N. (1996). *Experiential activities for intercultural learning.* Yarmouth. MD: Intercultural Press. Pg. 55

Stahl, G.K. (2001). Using assessment centers as tools for global leadership development: An exploratory study. In M.E. Mendenhall, T.M. Kühlmann, & G.K. Stahl (eds). Developing global business leaders. Westport, CT: Quorum Books: 197-210. Pg. 49

Takahashi, C., Yamagishi, T., Liu, J.H., Wang, F.X., Lin, Y.C. & Yu, S. (2008). The intercultural trust paradigm: Studying join cultural interaction and social exchange in real time over the Internet. *International Journal of Intercultural Relations,* 32, 215-228. doi:10.1016/j.ijintrel.2007.11.003. Pg. 85

Teagarden, M.B., & Gordon, G.D. (1995). Corporate selection strategies and expatriate manager success. In J. Selmer (Ed.) *Expatriate management: New ideas for international business*. Westport. Pg. 56

The Conference Board, Inc. 845 Third Avenue, New York, New York 10022-6679. Pg. 48

Torbert, W. (1987). Managing the Corporate Dream: Homewood, Illinois: Dow-Jones. Pgs. 17, 19

Training Magazine (2011) Developing Successful Global Leaders May/June, 2011. pp. 58-62. Pgs. 3, 48

Tucker, M.F., Benson, P.G., & Blanchard, F. (1978). *The measurement and prediction of overseas adjustment in the US Navy*. Denver, CO: Center for Research and Education. US Navy Bureau of Personnel Contract #N00600-73-D-070. Pg. 53

Tucker, M.F. (1982*). Your overseas suitability profile*. Boulder, CO: Tucker & Associates. Pg. 53

Tucker, M.F. (1983). *The overseas assignment inventory (OAI)*. Boulder, CO: Moran, Stahl & Boyer, International. Pg. 53

Tucker, M.F. (1994). *The overseas assignment inventory (OAI)*. Boulder, CO Tucker International, LLC. Pg. 53

Tucker, M.F., Bonial, R. & Lahti, K. (2004). The definition, measurement and prediction of intercultural adjustment and job performance among corporate expatriates. *International Journal of Intercultural Relations*, 28 221 – 251. Pg. 53

Tucker, M.F. (2008). *Managing projects across cultures*. In Chesley, J., Larson, W.J., McQuade, M., & Menrad, R.J: Applied project management for Space systems, McGraw-Hill. Pg. 56

Tucker, M.F., Bonial, R. & Lahti, K. (2004). The definition, measurement and prediction of intercultural adjustment and job performance among corporate expatriates. *International Journal of Intercultural Relations*, 28 221 – 251. Pg. 55

Tucker, M.F., Bonial, R., Vanhove, A., Kedharnath, U. (2014), **3**:127 – Leading across cultures in the human age: an empirical investigation of intercultural competency among global leaders. SpringerPlus - *a SpringerOpen Journal:* *http://www.springerplus.com/content/3/1/127*. Pgs. 8, 46

Vandenberg, R. J., & Lance, C.E. (2000). A review and synthesis of the measurement invariance literature: suggestions, practices, and recommendations for organizational research. *Organizational Research Methods, 3*, 4 – 69. Pg. 69

Walsh, D., Heyman, H. & Devany, M. (2008). *Lifetime learning survey: Summary of findings.* George Mason University. Pg. 55

Ward, C., & Kennedy, A. (1992). Locus of control, mood disturbance, and social difficulty during cross-cultural transitions. *International Journal of Intercultural Relations,* 16, 175 – 194. Pg. 59

Ward, C., & Kennedy, A. (1993). Psychological and socio-cultural adjustment during cross-cultural transitions: A comparison of secondary students overseas and at home. *International Journal of Psychology,* 28, 129 – 147. Pg. 59

Yamagishi, T. (2009, June 16). Trust in China and Japan: *Findings from "joint-cultural" experiments.* Paper presented at the 2009 IACM Conference, Kyoto, Japan. Pg. 85

Yamagishi, T., Cook, K.S., & Watabe, M. (1998). Uncertainty, trust, and commitment formation in the United States and Japan. *American Journal of Sociology,* 104, 165-194. doi:10.1086/210005. Pg. 85

Yamagishi, T., & Yamagishi, M. (1994). Trust and commitment in the United States and Japan. *Motivation and Emotion*, 18, 129-166. doi:10 1007/BF02249397. Pg. 85

Yellen, T.M.I., & Mumford, S.J. (1975). *The cross-cultural interaction inventory: Development of overseas criterion measures and items that differentiate between successful and unsuccessful adjusters.* San Diego, California: US Navy Personnel Research and Development Center. Pg. 53

Zaccaro, S.J. (2007). Trait-based perspectives of leadership. *American Psychologist, 62,* 6-16. Pgs. 51, 54, 90, 91

Zenger, John H., & Folkman, Joseph R. (2009). *The extraordinary leader:* McGraw-Hill. Pg. 58

ABOUT THE AUTHORS

Michael Tucker is the founder and President of Tucker International, a leader in the field of global talent assessment and development. He is an I/O Psychologist, Certified Management Consultant and Trustee, and a Fellow in the International Academy of Intercultural Research. He was the senior faculty member for the NASA International Project Management Program at the Kennedy Space Center. He has lived or worked in some 45 countries around the world, doing assessment, training and coaching global leaders and managers. Dr. Tucker has conducted and published large scale field research on the measurement and prediction of global performance. He spans the gap between research and practical application, authoring the OAI, TAP, GLTAP and the HV Model of Global Leadership Development. His writings include diversity in HR management, international project management, assessment and development for international assignments and ROI for intercultural assessment and training.

Lori Tucker-Eccher is the Director as well as Senior Assessor and Executive Coach at Tucker International. She lived as an expatriate as a child and has been involved in the field of intercultural communication in varying capacities for over 20 years.

She is the author of Tucker International's International Mobility Assessment IMA® and architect of Tucker Internationals ExpaTracks (an on-line expatriate candidate assessment tracking system). She is a certified assessor for the Overseas Assignment Inventory (OAI), the TAP® Assessment Profile and the Global Leader TAP® Assessment Profile (GLTAP). She has conducted well over 400 assessment feedback and coaching sessions with expatriates from multi-national companies taking on key leadership roles in over 25 countries. She is particularly interested in exploring research based applications for coaching and developing global leaders and more specifically the methods that inspire motivation for change.

Printed in the United States
By Bookmasters